God's Word and Our Words

Basic Homiletics

Ronald E. Sleeth

Foreword by Thomas G. Long

John Knox Press
ATLANTA

Library of Congress Cataloging-in-Publication Data

Sleeth, Ronald E. (Ronald Eugene), 1921-1985.
  God's word and our words.

  1. Preaching. I. Title.
BV4211.2.S545 1986   251   85-23777
ISBN 0-8042-1577-4

© copyright John Knox Press 1986
10 9 8 7 6 5 4 3 2 1
Printed in the United States of America
John Knox Press
Atlanta, Georgia 30365

Acknowledgment is made to the following sources:

To Abingdon Press for use of, adaptation of, and enlargement of ideas previously published in *Proclaiming the Word* (1964) and *Look Who's Talking* (1977).

To *The Circuit Rider* for use of material from Ronald E. Sleeth, "Wrestling with God's Angel," vol. 5, no. 1 (January 1981):14–15. Used with permission.

To *Encounter* for use of material from Charles E. Winquist, "The Sacrament of the Word of God," vol. 33, no. 3 (Summer 1972): 229. Used with permission.

To Houghton Mifflin Company for use of material from J.B.: A PLAY IN VERSE by Archibald MacLeish. Copyright © 1956, 1957, 1958 by Archibald MacLeish. Reprinted by permission of Houghton Mifflin Company.

To the Office of Worship, Presbyterian Church (U.S.A.) for use of ideas previously published as "Theology of the Word" reprinted from REFORMED LITURGY AND MUSIC, Volume XVII, No. 1, Winter 1983, by permission of the Office of Worship of the Presbyterian Church (U.S.A.).

To *Concilium* for use of material from Karl Rahner, "Demythologization and the Sermon," *The Renewal of Preaching: Theory and Practice*, Vol. 33 *Concilium*. Copyright 1968 by Paulist Fathers, Inc. and Stichting Concilium, all rights reserved. Used with permission of Paulist Press.

To *Perkins Journal* for use of material and elaboration of ideas set forth in the Peyton Lectures given at Perkins School of Theology in 1973 and published in abbreviated form by the *Perkins Journal*, Volume 30 (Summer 1977).

To *Pulpit Digest* for use of material in Harry Emerson Fosdick, "What Is the Matter with Preaching?" *Pulpit Digest* (September/October 1983).

To *Quarterly Review* for use of material in Lloyd Bailey, "From Text to Sermon: Reflections on Recent Discussion," reprinted from *Quarterly Review*, spring, 1981 with permission of The United Methodist Publishing House and the United Board of Higher Education and Ministry, © 1981.

To Jack Stotts for use of material from his charge to Donald M. Wardlaw upon his installation as James G. K. McClure Professor of Preaching and Worship at McCormick Theological Seminary on May 17, 1979.

Preface

God's Word and Our Words purports to be a comprehensive book on homiletics within a brief scope. This book differentiates itself from other works on preaching by covering some areas not usually found in general books on pulpit proclamation. For example, *God's Word and Our Words*, among other things, covers three important but often neglected areas: first, preaching is inextricably tied to the nature of the gospel itself; second, preaching today is set in the context of its history; the roots of Christian preaching are seen in the synagogue, in Greek and Roman rhetoric, and in the uniqueness of the Christian gospel; third, preaching is seen also in the light of contemporary communication theories.

In addition, the book attempts to avoid being either another "How to" book on preaching methods or a theoretical treatise on the theory of preaching. It lays out basic homiletical principles and indicates how those principles could be incorporated in the various facets of the preaching act. Rather than discussing specific aspects of preaching chapter by chapter, i.e., illustrations, conclusions, introductions, I have placed these functions in the context of basic homiletical and rhetorical principles which undergird specific functions but are also applicable to wider dimensions of the sermon. In short, the book is theoretical in terms of principles and practical in terms of methodology. Though the book can serve as a basic text in homiletics in a theological seminary, it will also appeal to the parish minister, who would like to reinforce the centrality of the pulpit and to consider new dimensions of proclamation of which he or she has not been aware.

Off and on I have remarked that I learn from one student generation and write for the next. The dedication of this book to students who have been in my classroom through the years attests to that fact. Other books written earlier will reflect the growth of a developing theory during a good many years. *Persuasive Preaching* (New York: Harper & Row, 1956 [two editions] and reprinted by Berrien Springs, MI: Andrews University Press, 1981) represented a bridge between communication studies, especially persuasion, and homiletics. *Proclaiming the*

Word (Nashville: Abingdon, 1964) was an attempt to elucidate a theory of preaching reflecting the post-war biblical/theological renaissance. *Look Who's Talking* (Nashville: Abingdon, 1977), written especially for laypersons, was the application of communicative and rhetorical principles for lay speaking.

Some of the material in this book was given earlier in a different form as the Peyton Lectures at the Perkins School of Theology, Southern Methodist University, in 1973. I am still grateful to the administration, the students, the alumni, and my colleagues at Perkins for the honor of that invitation. *The Perkins Journal,* Summer 1977, reprinted a condensation of those lectures. I am thankful for the permission to incorporate certain sections of these lectures in this manuscript. The essence of Chapter 1 appeared in *Reformed Liturgy and Music* in the winter issue, 1983.

I am indebted to my former student assistant, Dr. Roger Fallot, for reading the manuscript in the early stages. His criticisms and suggestions are reflected in the book in many ways. Natalie Sleeth, my wife, read the manuscript with a grammarian's eye and with loving care. Mrs. Margaret Manion typed the manuscript, and Susan Ortman Goering helped in many ways, including compiling the index.

—Ronald E. Sleeth

Foreword

A keen sense of the theological character of preaching has always been the hallmark of Ronald Sleeth's career as a preacher and a teacher of preachers. In a time when much creative effort is expended on matters of preaching style, rhetorical finesse, and innovative sermon structures, Ronald Sleeth has consistently reminded us that preaching disintegrates into mere technique unless we ask the theological question before we ask the methodological question. "Proclamation is a theological act," he claims. "The *why* of preaching is as important as the *what* and *how*."

The present volume is, in essence, a description of what happens to the practice of preaching when the theological character of preaching is taken seriously. Viewed from this perspective, preaching cannot be seen as an activity which is only "about" God's Word, or "based upon" God's Word; preaching *is* the Word, and, as such, is a dynamic event for those who hear and a crisis of faith for those who preach. "To put it starkly," Sleeth tells us, "many preachers' malaise about the preaching task . . . is their own struggle with revelation—or even faith."

Since preaching is continuous with revelation, and revelation occurs in and through history, Sleeth is concerned to explore the historical origins and development of preaching. Over against those who would too easily identify the Christian preacher with the Hebrew prophet and those who would too easily separate the development of preaching from the forces of classical rhetoric, Sleeth advances a more accurate picture of the preaching stream flowing from the confluence of three tributaries: classical rhetoric, Jewish tradition, and the character of the gospel itself. This allows him to avoid the false dichotomies of prophetic preaching versus priestly preaching, biblical exposition versus rhetorical discourse, and gospel proclamation versus ethical instruction. Preaching is *both* prophetic *and* priestly. It is at one and the same time biblically based *and* rhetorically sensitive. It is kerygmatic proclamation which, by nature, *includes* explicit ethical mandates.

While no enemy of the artistic, creative, and metaphorical impulses

in preaching, Sleeth is determined to root out the fuzziness and un-
clarity which often hide behind an aesthetic facade. Indeed, he goes a
long way toward reclaiming the power of the clear thesis and the linear
structure in sermons. He is not insistent upon any single form or shape
for sermons, but he does demand that sermons have a form which is
coherent and which provides for movement and progression. Sleeth's
concern at this point does not grow out of a reverence for classical rhetoric or traditional homiletics but rather springs from his theological
conviction that God's Word expresses itself *clearly*. If preachers do not
have clarity, they are like "a sounding brass and tinkling cymbal."

The theological character of preaching has implications not only for
the sermon but also for the preacher. While the older homiletical texts
gave great attention to the person and character of the preacher, more
recent treatments have tended to minimize, or even to ignore, this, shy-
ing away from any notion that the preacher should stand "apart from"
or (even worse) "above" the hearers. While carefully avoiding any
hierarchical or morally-superior views of the preacher, Sleeth returns to
the discussion of the person of the preacher with fresh insight and theological conviction. He boldly and controversially states that "the Word
becomes flesh in the person and words of the preacher" and develops
this theological theme into a "middle path" for the preacher who
wishes to avoid, on the one hand, trying to hide the self in preaching,
and, on the other, overemphasizing one's own life, experience, and
personality.

It is Sleeth's theological orientation which presses him beyond the
written words of the sermon manuscript to a reclaiming of the essentially *oral* character of gospel proclamation. The gospel is an urgent
message, and the spoken word "is the form into which an urgent message most naturally flows." God's Word is not propositional truth; it is
an event in time expressed in speech, a "word which addresses man
and woman as cultural beings." Because God's Word finds expression
in human speech, it can never be confined to the cultus, but moves to
embrace the world. It can never be frozen and codified into a set of
principles or eternal verities but remains alive, active, dynamic.

"Who dares, who can, preach, knowing what preaching is?" asked
Karl Barth, and this book exposes us anew to the depth and crisis of
that question. In that sense, this is a sobering book, in many ways a

frightening one. No preacher who reads this book can go casually or thoughtlessly into the pulpit again. We are told here what preaching is, and all of our efforts to reduce its size, to bring the task into manageable proportions, are thrown into judgment. This book is also full of confidence, encouragement, hope, and joy about the ministry of preaching. "There is nothing," Barth went on to say, "more important, more urgent, more helpful, more redemptive, and more salutary . . . than the speaking and the hearing of the Word of God." Ronald Sleeth wants us to recover both the mystery and the power of the act of preaching, and it is to that purpose that this volume is shaped.

—Thomas G. Long
Princeton Theological Seminary

Contents

... wrestle with words so that they may serve whole-
ness. . . . Teach us so to speak and to be that our words
will serve the purpose of a Word whose work and calling
was reconciliation of the whole creation. . . . Help us to
love and therefore to wrestle with the Word and the words.

—Jack L. Stotts

When you focus all your thought
  on the power of the words,
    you may begin to see the sparks of light
    that shine within them.
The sacred letters are the chambers
  into which God pours His flowing light.
The lights within each letter, as they touch,
  ignite one another,
    and new lights are born.

It is of this the Psalmist says:
  "Light is sown for the righteous,
    and joy for the upright in heart."

—*Your Word Is Fire: The Hasidic Masters on Contempla-
tive Prayer*, edited and translated by Arthur Green and
Barry W. Holtz (New York: Paulist Press, 1977), p. 46.

1

Theology
of the Word

To understand preaching correctly, one needs to see that Christian proclamation is a theological act. The *why* of preaching is as important as the *what* and *how*. As crucial as it is to have something to communicate and to know how to do that effectively, the decisive issue is to know why *preaching* the gospel has been so inextricably tied to the gospel itself. From its beginnings, the church has persisted in affirming that the telling of the story has an integral relationship to the story itself. One could say that the preaching of the gospel is part of the gospel. Christian discourse cannot be seen simply as sacred rhetoric or as a public speech on a religious theme. Preaching is part and parcel of what it proclaims. As important as it is to have a message and to be able to develop God-given skills, the basis of Christian preaching rests firmly on a theological foundation.

The tremendous claim of this theological foundation is that the

Word of God is the basis of the preacher's authority. Historically and theologically, the church has always claimed that in some unique way the preacher is proclaiming a Word from God and is God's spokesperson. One scholar has said, "For [Luther] preaching was the veritable Word of God Himself, and, as such, occupied the central position in the Church."[1] Or, to put it more succinctly, the preaching of the Word *is* the Word. One might suggest that Luther seemed to move the doctrine of transubstantiation from the altar to the pulpit. In his commentary on Genesis, he affirmed that "it is in the Word alone that the bread is the body of Christ, that the wine is the blood of Christ."[2]

Such a "high" view of preaching may seem encased in a type of Reformation scholasticism. Yet, even in a more recent time those with the same view make a similar affirmation, though in different words. Theodore Wedel states:

> For, even in weakness, the sermon, if true to its calling, performs a kind of transubstantiation miracle—a transubstantiation in time though not in space. The sermon contemporizes the gospel—a gospel which, as merely read gospel, might have remained safely entombed in the church's historical archives. From a *then*, or "once upon a time," it confronts the hearer with a *now*.[3]

Luther went so far as to affirm that the Holy Spirit was present in the Word and there only. In one of his Wittenberg sermons he mentions that after he has preached and while the Word is working its work in the hearts and lives of the believers, he can go have a beer with his friends Amsdorf and Philipp. Zwingli argued that the spirit was not in the Word solely, but even apart from it, and spoke directly to the soul. Calvin, in a mediating stance, believed in the real presence of the Holy Spirit in the Word and in the inner witness of the Holy Spirit in the heart of the believer.

Though today we may be of a variety of theological persuasions, it is nevertheless true that whatever our stance or denomination, historically—in one form or another—it has been averred that the Word cannot be separated from its proclamation. Or, to put it another way, the gospel is a preached gospel. Preaching, however bad the practice of it has been, has remained central in the Protestant tradition. Protestants, however, should never feel proprietary or smug about being custodians of proclamation. As we shall see, the historical roots of preaching go far back into our religious history. Preaching flowered greatly in the fourth century and was never completely dormant through the ages between the fourth and the sixteenth centuries. Though one might assume the Catholic tradition has minimized preaching to the elevation of the mass, that very tradition was the carrier of preaching long before the Reformation. In our modern period Vatican II re-emphasized preaching in the Constitution on the Sacred Liturgy:

> By means of the homily the mysteries of the faith and the guiding principles of the Christian life are expounded from the sacred text during the course of the liturgical year. The homily, therefore, is to be highly esteemed as part of the liturgy itself; in fact, at those Masses which are celebrated with the assistance of the people on Sundays and feasts of obligation, it should not be omitted except for a serious reason.[4]

Jaroslav Pelikan, in commenting upon the Vatican II document, says:

> Of particular moment for the recovery of the centrality of Scripture in worship is the restoration of preaching. The theological basis for that restoration is the doctrine that Christ is present not only in the sacraments, but also "in His word, since it is He Himself who speaks when the holy Scriptures are read in the church."[5]

Whatever the branch of Christendom, then, the preaching of the Word has been and remains a central affirmation of the church. Indeed, the church itself has been defined in those terms:

> The visible Church of Christ is a congregation of faithful men in which *the pure Word of God is preached*, and the Sacraments duly administered (italics mine).[6]

Ordination vows are similar. The United Methodist service, which would have corollaries in other groups, charges the deacons:

> In the name of our Lord Jesus Christ, you have been ordained deacons in the Church of God. Faithfully exercise the authority given you by God and the Church to proclaim God's Word and to serve God's people.[7]

For the elders:

> In the name of our Lord Jesus Christ you have been ordained elders in the Church of God. Faithfully exercise the authority given you by God and the Church to proclaim Good News in Word and Sacrament.[8]

Though ordination vows differ from one tradition to another, a universality exists in the seriousness with which the vows of preaching are bestowed.

Unless the phrase "preach the Word" remains a verbal shibboleth, one must come to terms with the *Word* and what it means to preach the Word of God. Certainly any interpretation of that term would depend upon one's theological stance, and universality in a pluralistic Christian world is hard to achieve. At the same time there is a wide spectrum of the Christian body that makes the tremendous, awe-inspiring claim that the Word of God is the basis for the preacher's authority when he or she stands in the pulpit. As already indicated, it would be an error to assume that this "high" view of the preaching role is to be associated only with the Reformers or with those who stand in the Reformed theological tradition.

In our day, with emphasis upon story, parable, narrative, telling, and witness, the Christian tradition of "telling the story of Jesus" has received renewed emphasis from all quarters of the Christian church. Indeed, this "new dimension" is often discussed apart from any specific theological grounding. The point is not the denomination, confession, or creed, but the universality within the church of the decisive importance of the spoken word in relation to the Word of God. William Willimon states the contemporaneity of this point helpfully:

> The Word of God is not something encased in our tradition. It must be spoken and it must be spoken in our time and place by men and women who are called into the service of that word. There is no church where the Name is not named, the story is not told, the word is not spoken.[9]

Such a mandate can be stated in our day as simply as saying the words of the old hymn, "Tell Me the Old, Old Story."

If the phrase "Word of God" becomes more than a theological verbalism, then we must move one step further to see upon what that claim rests. To say that one proclaims the Word of God is incredible enough, but that claim rests upon another incredible claim—revelation. The preacher's authority for preaching the Word is that this Word has come to him or her. Historically, we have affirmed that God is revealed in creation, Scriptures, Jesus Christ, sacraments, the church, the apostles, and the mouths of preachers. For the Christian, this revelation comes primarily in Jesus the Christ. In short, there is a correlation between preaching the Word of God and a belief about revelation.

In a sense, the relationship between revelation and preaching may point to one of the significant concerns about preaching in this or any day. To state it starkly, many preachers' malaise about the preaching task is not really their concern with the effectiveness of preaching to touch lives, but it is rather their own struggle with revelation—or even faith. To say it another way, some reject preaching for the wrong reasons. They may say that it is not effective communication——not dialogic enough, too rationalistic, too authoritarian—while the real reason could be that they no longer believe a Word has come to them. Some wonder if anything or anyone is "coming through." They may no longer feel that God has "spoken" or is "speaking."

Revelation, of course, as a theological concept goes far beyond the province of these pages. It may be that revelation has too often been associated with Reformation theology, and therefore, the nature of preaching has been too stringently defined in that light. Or, perhaps the concept of revelation has changed or is changing constantly. We cannot speak of revelation as we once did. To some, the underlying assumption of the historic doctrine of revelation simply cannot be assumed any more. It may have rested upon a wholly-other, transcendent God whom we no longer accept. For some, it may mean that the death-of-God movement had more effect than was first thought. It was believed by many that the movement really had little impact philosophically or theologically. Perhaps it did, pragmatically. Preachers may feel that they are bereft of a Word because there is nothing "out there." To others, the primary questions are no longer connected with God but with the human situation. Theological questions have been replaced with anthropological ones. Still others affirm that the Word of God can no longer be capitalized and that revelation has rested upon a static view of a *kerygma* which somehow is given to the preacher. Whatever the reason, revelation and its ambiguities may be the real reason preachers have trouble coming to terms with the pulpit and the preaching office—especially when it is affirmed that preaching is proclaiming the Word of God.

Still, for one to affirm that he or she is preaching the Word of God assumes that one has a word from God to preach; hence revelation. Revelation, however, does not need to be seen as esoteric, static, or as a theology to be delivered. What Richard Niebuhr said for theology would be applicable for preaching. "Theology [preaching too?], then, must begin in Christian history and with Christian history because it has no other choice; in this sense it is forced to begin with revelation, meaning by that word *simply historic faith*"(italics mine).[10] That historic faith is telling the story of our history, a story not so much of our seeking God but of God seeking us. This history is not static, however. "The revelation of God is not a possession but an event, which happens over and over again when we remember the illuminating center of our history."[11] Many speak of preaching as Event an encounter which can join the congregation and the Word of God r a dynamic happening. Such an Event is not the transmission of a ɔody of knowledge, or a verbal formula, or a word about salvation. As Fred Craddock reminds us, " 'Preaching' can be properly defined as both 'that which is preached' and 'the act of presenting the Gospel.' "[12] Or as Dominico Grasso puts it, preaching "is Revelation in transmission."[13] The Event of preaching is itself salvific; the illuminating moment can happen there; the Word is efficacious in that moment. Ebeling, who has emphasized the Word-Event nature of preaching, writes of the importance of revelation and preaching:

> God's Word is expressed anew only when it is heard anew, with tense attention to how the traditional Word manages to make itself understood in the real circumstances to which our lives are exposed.[14]

The correlation between revelation and preaching, then, can be seen in a variety of expressions and led Tom Oden in a recent book to assert that "the authority of the preacher is grounded in the depth of the speaker's correspondence with the revealed word."[15]

What we affirm about preaching being an Event implies that salvation happens *now*, and happens again and again. Though we acknowledge that preaching in one sense is telling the old, old story, it is a now-story, too. We do not have to use existentialist categories alone to aver that the message of the gospel is tied to the preaching of it. What Bultmann calls the "salvation-occurrence" is present *now* in preaching. Many preachers sense the difference between *preaching* the gospel and preaching about the gospel: the difference between preaching about historical happenings and preaching Scripture in a way that explains and gives meaning to current happenings. The faith once delivered to the saints is also delivered to us, whereby our historic faith becomes our present history. That is, of course, good news to the congregations who wish to know that Christ is risen and alive today. It should also be good news for preachers to know that the Word they preach is alive and dynamic and that it can be a means of grace.

2

Preaching's Debt
to the Old Testament

Christian preaching has its origin in three distinct roots: classical rhetoric (both Greek and Roman), the Jewish tradition from which it sprang, and the Christian gospel itself. These three, each with its own particular emphasis, fused to become the central tradition for Christian proclamation.

The most obvious strain in Christian preaching comes from the Old Testament. The first Christians, being Jews, took over from their historic faith many of their worship practices and adapted them to their newfound one. Worship, rites, and liturgy became part of the new religion, even though reinterpreted. Jesus himself saw his role as the fulfiller of the Hebrews' expectations, not as the destroyer of the historic faith of which he was a descendant.

Yet, there have always been some who see a radical discontinuity between the Old Testament and the New, between Hebrew religion and the Christian faith. Throughout the history of Christian preaching there always have been those who attempt to separate Christianity from its Jewishness. A. E. Garvie, while acknowledging a connection between Hebrew prophecy and preaching, nevertheless, affirms that "The history of Christian preaching must begin with Him who is both the model and the message, Jesus Christ the Lord," thus, largely ignoring Jewish worship and completely overlooking the influence of classical rhetoric.[1] Nevertheless, the preponderance of evidence is that not only Christian faith but also Christian preaching is related to earlier forms of worship, too. Dargan states unequivocally that "there was a clearly defined basis for Christian preaching in the sacred speech of that people from whom in the divine ordering of events Christianity sprang."[2] T. Harwood Pattison, of the same period as Dargan, seeing this connection, clearly begins his history with the Old Testament prophets and specifically decries those who see the Christian preacher apart from the Hebrew roots.[3] Brilioth sees the Christian preacher in relation to both the synagogue service and, even more important, to Old Testament prophecy.[4] One need not belabor the point to make it clear that just as Jesus' faith was an extension of the faith of his forebears, so is preaching inextricably tied to the Hebrew faith which preceded it.

Indeed, as over against those who see in Christian preaching a unique act which began only with the *kerygma*, we can observe what might be called a Jewish backlash. There are those in that tradition who, far from admitting the uniqueness of *preaching* as a Christian act, rather affirm that Christians took over what was a well-defined practice and claimed it as their own. One scholar states, "that to preach was essentially and historically a Jewish practice, which long antedated the rise of Christianity. The sermon was not an accretion upon the synagogue service, but an indispensable factor in carrying out the object for which that institution had been created."[5] Such an affirmation balances those who claim a distinct role for the origin of Christian preaching.

After facing the evidence that demonstrates the integral relationship between preaching and its Old Testament predecessors, one proceeds to see what these early evidences looked like and what were the strains of development into the Christian period. One of the first ways to relate Christian preaching to Old Testament sources is to study the portions of the Old Testament which could have been oral—speeches and "sermons." Dargan,[6] to name only one, has attempted to isolate those passages in the Old Testament which might have been "sermons": Moses (pleading lack of eloquence), Job's questioners, Judah before Joseph in Egypt, Deuteronomy are all given as examples to show that the sermonic form was inherent in the Old Testament. As enticing as this approach might be, the perils are real, too. First, there is always the danger of "modernizing" the Old Testament, seeking to make it a pattern for our preaching (e.g., Nathan's judgment of David as a model for indirect discourse). Second, it would take a high degree of biblical scholarship to isolate those portions of Scripture which were "oral" in origin. Finally, even if we could signify portions of Scripture which were "oral," we would still be a long way from our purpose: to examine the development of preaching from its sources. Such an approach leads us more to the *nature* of Old Testament preaching and the *forms* which we can discern than to bits and pieces or excerpts which are tenuous at best.

We are on much safer ground when we turn to something more easily definable, such as the prophetic tradition, although even in this area we have a host of problems. Nevertheless, Broadus states categorically that "the prophets were preachers."[7] He goes on to point out that the New Testament minister is not a priest but a prophet. It is from this tradition that the preacher springs—minus, of course, the predictive elements often associated with Old Testament prophecy. It is this theory that has long associated the preacher with the prophet and seeks to see in the prophetic utterances both the content of the "sermons" and the prophets' methods as the model for subsequent "prophets" or "preachers." Thus, Samuel, Isaiah, Hosea, Micah, Amos, for example, are really precursors of Christian preachers. Jesus, himself, stands in this same line. These were the men who opened their addresses with, "Thus says the Lord," who spoke directly to kings, and who pleaded, warned, rebuked, or encouraged both peoples and their leaders. Some even begin this prophetic tradition with Moses. Says Ker, "It is in every way likely that after Moses there was a continuous class of religious teachers, whose work it was to instruct and warn."[8] It would be both interesting and instructive to follow this line of development with more thoroughness. For example, it would be enticing to view the specific work of the prophets, the various prophets of each period, and the content of their prophecy. Sufficient for our purposes, however, is to state that later theories of Christian preaching have some basis for relating the act of preaching to the prophets in at least two ways.

First of all, proclaiming that Scripture *is* the Word of God has some basis in the prophets' claim that they spoke the Word of God. Or, at least, that as God speaks in events, the prophet interprets God's words to the people (Num. 12:2).[9] That the prophet claimed to speak for God is undoubtedly true, and this authority is the same one that preaching—in one way or another—has claimed ever since. The second prophetic aspect in which we see a direct relationship to the preaching that followed is the nature of the message they taught ("preached"). It is often the pattern for effective and contemporary preaching: the basis in the past, the facts of divine history—what God has done. Then, the past brought to bear on the present—what God is doing. And, finally, the future—what God will do.

Yet, in spite of the visible similarities between the prophetic tradition and the later role of the Christian preacher, the synonymous use of the two interchangeably raises a host of questions. Apart from the usual simplistic association of the prophet with the prophetic or social gospel preacher, there is the more basic one of the too easy separation of prophet and priest. Thus, the use of the term *prophet* as more appropriate to the Christian minister as preacher than the term *priest*, for example. Indeed, the term priest is often used pejoratively in contradistinction to the preacher as prophet. Broadus, speaking for many historians in the field of preaching, declares, "You are no doubt all aware that the New Testament minister corresponds not at all to the Old Testament *priest*, but in important respects to the Old Testament *prophet*."[10]

However, it is becoming more and more clear that the separation of these two roles is a false dichotomy. Davidson[11] suggests that this distinction between a prophet and priest is too rigid. In early times the distinction between the two does not seem to have been sharp. Samuel was both a priest and a prophet. Jeremiah and Ezekiel both came out of priestly families. This connection of priests and prophets was always close (Isa. 8:12). H. H. Rowley argues that "there is ample evidence that prophets function beside priests in the worship."[12] Some scholars feel that Ezra, whom we usually think of in the priestly tradition, was the first "preacher." It was Ezra who interpreted the texts while the prophets were often simply oracles, speaking of things within them. This very important distinction between interpreting texts and "speaking of things within" is still a current discussion in defining the nature of preaching.

It has often been assumed that, just as the prophet is the more natural ancestor of the preacher than the priest, so is the synagogue a more natural parent of the preaching service than is the temple. What is the relation between the synagogue and the temple and how much is the former a precursor of the Christian service, including the role of the preacher within that service? In other words, is there a direct line of development from the prophet→to the synagogue→to the Christian service of proclamation as over against priest→temple→sacrifice? Such a distinction has often been stated as the basis for the differences between the Protestant and Catholic traditions. Also, it has served to define the specific roles of a modern priest or preacher. Historically, and even currently, the difference tends to be stated, "the priest interprets man to God, the prophet God to man."[13] We have seen the danger of this generalization and even have seen that one scholar affirms that the prophets and priests may have functioned side by side in the service. Indeed, the distinction between the two becomes even more blurred when we note that there were "cultic prophets, with a defined place in the cultus of the Temple."[14] Instead of the usual division spoken of above, it might very well be affirmed with Rowley: "For the prophet was not only the man who brought the word of God to man. He was also the spokesman of man to God, and as intercessor he figures frequently in the Old Testament."[15]

We can and should avoid—as with priest and prophet—any attempt to divide the temple and the synagogue. Just as we have seen that both prophets and priests officiated in the temple, so it would be false to trace two distinct lines of development indicating different religious traditions. For the Jew, it was not either synagogue or temple, but synagogue *and* temple. The synagogue, whose relationship to Christian worship is easy to see later, has a somewhat vague origin. H. H. Rowley, after discussing the various theories of the origin of the synagogue, states as a conclusion that "the Synagogue arose among the exiles in Babylon, who began, perhaps first in one another's homes, to meet to keep their faith alive."[16] The intention was not to substitute the synagogue for the temple; it was simply to keep the faith alive while removed from the Jerusalem temple. So while in the temple the sacrifices of the faith were performed, the synagogues arose, as Herbert says, "to integrate the Jewish community to that worship."[17] Yet, since the synagogue was not to take the place of the temple, it is only natural that the form of worship which sprang up was different.

It is this synagogue service which concerns us here as a forerunner to Christian worship and preaching. Of the similarities there can be no doubt, even though as we have indicated there are still those who discount the Jewish roots of Christian preaching. By looking at the synagogue service it is easy to see the aspects of worship which were later taken over by the Christian church, especially in regard to preaching. Brilioth states the matter clearly (although his dating may be questionable): "If by preaching we mean the exposition of a holy writing as an act of the cult, we can hardly identify the Jewish sermon until post-exilic times. It is in the synagogue service that the Jewish sermon assumes its form."[18] This is not to say that there was not preaching in some form before post-exilic times. We have already seen that some identify "preaching" from the earliest Old Testament period. Brilioth himself identifies preaching in the broadest sense with earlier dates. He particularly links preaching to the prophetic tradition, as we have seen others do. To him, "a clear line extends from Old Testament prophecy to the sermon in the Church."[19]

It is exceedingly difficult to pin down the elements of the Jewish synagogue service from its earliest roots. The sources are sketchy, and we are often in the realm of speculation. Many scholars, however, have their theories of what took place. In speaking of the reading of Scripture—which always occurred—Oesterly describes the service as follows:

> Torah (Pentateuch) was read on Mondays and Thursdays, and on feast-days. On Sabbaths and feast-days there was read, in addition to the Pentateuch lesson, a passage from the prophetic books. These were, of course, always read in Hebrew; but there followed immediately a translation in the vernacular, and an *explanatory exposition* (italics mine).[20]

A biblical reference to this service is suggested in Nehemiah 8:8: "And they read from the book, from the law of God, clearly; and they gave the sense, so that the people understood the reading." Such an explanation of Scripture is believed to be the first step in the preaching of the Word. From this practice arose Targums (explanatory translations of the Hebrew Scriptures into the vernacular) which, in reality, are sermons in germ. Thus, centuries before the Christian era, the custom of public reading of the Pentateuch, followed by an exposition, was in vogue. The same became true for the reading and exposition of prophetic books—although the latter practice did not begin until approximately two centuries before the Christian era. To sum up this development, Oesterly explains that there were four elements in worship: the reading of Scripture, the preaching of the Word, prayers, and psalmody. These become the essential and integral parts of the synagogue liturgy.[21]

Though such an explanation suggests uniformity in synagogue worship, there were variations. Brilioth goes so far as to base his history of preaching upon the pattern of Jesus speaking in the synagogue from the familiar passage in Isaiah 61 and considers this a literal model for subsequent preachers. He also infers that this pattern was normative for the synagogue. From this Gospel report he even deduces such liturgical practices as Jesus being seated in the synagogue reading from Isaiah becoming the norm that was followed by the bishops in the early church. Whether the report of Jesus' commission in the Gospels can be taken as a faithful blueprint of a historical occasion and as a guide for modern preaching is beside the point here. What is important is that the synagogue setting for Scripture and exposition was carried into the Christian era and was a common experience for the practicing Jew—and thus for the first Christians.

Whereas our main attention should not be focused on such matters as architecture, a writer like Pattison describes the setting of the synagogue in terms which make it a natural setting for preaching. It is described as being oblong, with a low platform at one end with a desk for the leader—and there the Scriptures were read and the discourse delivered. Behind stood the ark with the copies of the law.[22] A more contemporary scholar, H. H. Rowley, spends an illuminating chapter on the nature of synagogue worship and relates it all to the Christian church by affirming that, "the Church continued to use the same type of worship, including prayer, the reading of Scripture, and exposition."[23] Hans Lietzmann has observed that "as a rule, the Christian churches soon adopted the forms used by the Hellenistic synagogues, and they constitute the foundation of Christian public worship to the present day."[24]

There seems to be no serious reason to doubt these observations of the indebtedness to the synagogue of the early Christians. After all, they were following the faith and practice of their ancestors, and in spite of any radical attempts at discontinuity, Jesus himself saw himself in the prophetic strain of the Jewish tradition. That he was unique, and that preaching which emanated from his followers was different, goes without saying. But as he saw his task, not to abrogate the law, but to fulfill it, so we can see that one major source of preaching was this tradition wherein God had been working through people whose understanding of God's will was to proclaim that Word to others. Someone has said that a Christian must first of all be a good Jew before he or she can be a good Christian. Whether or not that is a theological axiom or a manifestation of Christian experience, it is certainly true that in the history of preaching one large segment of our heritage is the Jewish faith which preceded us.

3

Preaching's Debt
to the Greeks and Romans

If the first important influence on Christian preaching was the Hebrew religion and its cultic practices, the second was classical rhetoric—both Greek and Roman. Classical rhetoric in the history of Christian preaching cannot be overemphasized, though, as in the case of the Old Testament roots for Christian preaching, there are contemporary writers who disparage rhetoric and lay at its feet many of the problems that beset modern-day preaching.[1] The kindest thing to be said concerning these critics is that they are often inadequate students of the history of preaching. Further, few are knowledgeable concerning classical rhetoric. This is not to say that the incorporation of rhetoric into the Christian church did not bring with it many difficulties. The absorption of Green and Roman rhetoric into the Christian framework did cause problems, but its influence cannot be denied, and its service to the Christian gospel cannot be underestimated.

Rhetoric was born and developed in Greece. Dargan believes that the art of rhetoric flourished there due to the political situation of that culture. The other three great civilizations of the ancient world did not contribute to the development of oratory, for these—Egyptian, Assyrian, Persian—were all despotic in government, and such is not the climate for eloquence. On the other hand, the Greeks brought rhetoric and oratory to their culmination. The speeches employed in the Homeric poems show that in the earliest times the Greeks prized the gift of eloquence. Five reasons are given for this development: (1) the growth of political freedom, (2) the early and vigorous development of dialectical philosophy, (3) the cultivation and excellence of art and literature, (4) an imaginative and lively intellect, and (5) the flexible and powerful language of the Greeks.[2]

Whatever the reasons, rhetoric developed most fully in Athens. It culminated in Demosthenes, the greatest of the ancient orators. It is significant that both Aristotle and Demosthenes died in 322 B.C.; for, if Demosthenes was the greatest practitioner of the art of oratory, Aristotle was the greatest theorist. It was he who developed principles for the practice of rhetoric and these ideas, with variations, of course, have persisted to the present day in communication theory. His theories were incorporated into the development of Christian preaching, as we shall see. The passing of Aristotle and Demosthenes, coupled with the political overthrow of Greece, caused an ebb in the importance of oratory, but its lasting imprint had been made. Although it reached its climax with Demosthenes, it had a much earlier beginning with the Sophists.

Today, sophistry has bad connotations, meaning fallacious reasoning. In the beginning, the Sophists (around 460 B.C.) were itinerant teachers who taught, wrote, and spoke about morals, rhetoric, citizenship, and philosophy. They were in conflict with the philosophers. Plato, especially, maligned the Sophists for their relativism and skepticism. They did not believe in absolute truth; yet, they taught "doctrines" concerning philosophy, ethics, and rhetoric. In so doing, they were regarded as destroyers of the accepted philosophy. Basically, they were not "content-centered" but were professional teachers who wrote texts and gave lessons in public address. Further, they wrote manuals of rhetoric designed to "get results." They were the original how-to-win-friends-and-influence-people school. They were used by the novices who needed to speak in public (law courts, legislative assemblies, and ceremonial speaking) and, as we have seen, they taught rhetoric and gave speeches themselves.[3]

Not all the rhetoricians of this period are easy to classify, however. Isocrates, for example, is sometimes considered to be a Sophist, for he was practical and took money for the teaching of rhetoric. He also rivaled the philosophers. He criticized the Sophists, by recognizing their limitations and by developing his teaching along the lines of the philosophers. He established the first permanent school of rhetoric in Athens, and many of his methods and ideals are found in Cicero. Isocrates particularly emphasized the need for good character in the speaker and saw rhetoric as the core of the general culture.

On the whole, the Sophists were maligned for the following reasons: (1) a complete indifference to truth, (2) an aversion to all patient, scientific research, (3) a fondness for the "jingle" of words, (4) anxiety for persuasion rather than knowledge, and (5) attachment to appearances and to the superficial, immediate effect.[4] To affirm these criticisms does not minimize the undoubted effects of the Sophists in the history of rhetoric, for they did a great deal for the art of discourse—both theory and practice. They were the precursors of the later and more philosophic-minded rhetoricians. In other words, Athens formed her rhetoric under the direction of the Sophists, and they helped teach the orators the art of writing.

To see the development of rhetoric and its later impingement upon the Christian tradition, we need to see something of the struggle within the development of rhetorical theory itself. On the one hand, we have indicated briefly the nature of the sophistic movement and the "practical" emphasis within rhetoric. On the other hand, and at the other extreme, stand the philosophers symbolized by Plato. Plato's indictment of rhetoric was twofold: (1) the rhetoric he saw was superficial, and he naturally rebelled against the sophistic rhetoric then in practice; (2) he objected to rhetoric on more philosophical grounds.[5] He contended that in an "ideal" society there would be no need for rhetoric. To oversimplify, Plato felt that rhetoric was persuasion and in his society "truth" would prevail by its own impact. As to oratory, he believed that a possessor of knowledge, by virtue of this knowledge, would be able to speak effectively.

These two extremes, which have their counterparts even today, were the background against which we must see the development of Aristotelian rhetoric.[6] Aristotle stood midway between Plato and the Sophists. He argued that in a democratic society there was a need for advocacy. That is, instead of a philosophy class making decisions on the one hand, or people with no opinions on the other, a democracy was made up of contending points-of-view, each vying with one another for supremacy. It was in such a society that Aristotle saw the need for rhetoric—as a means of persuasion and advocacy. He was critical of the Sophists, too, for they lacked a rhetoric based upon sound principles. His attempt was to reduce rhetorical theory to first principles—a philosophic rhetoric. As C. S. Baldwin writes, "Rhetoric, in the philosophy of Aristotle, is essentially giving effectiveness to truth."[7]

For our purposes, we can ignore all of Aristotle's works on philosophy and physical sciences and concentrate on his *Rhetoric*. This ancient book, which has been a primer for the rhetoricians and even homileticians, sets forth clearly (though often derivatively and unrecognized) Aristotle's theory of rhetoric. As Christian preachers we are all indebted to his work. His emphasis upon *ethos*, the factor of the character of the speaker in the process of persuasion, would be only one example of the indebtedness the modern preacher has to classical rhetoric, and Aristotle in particular.

The strains of classical oratory are seen in the earliest of the Christian churches. Indeed, rhetoric also affected the Jews—especially those in the diaspora. Hartwig Thyen[8] has written of the Hellenistic Jews that the form and spirit of Hellenistic Jewish preaching in the diaspora came from two sources: (1) Old Testament Jewish life as inherited from Palestine; (2) the popular Greek philosophers who, of course, reflected Greek culture. Indeed, the cynic-stoic diatribe—one branch of classical rhetoric—shaped the synagogue homily. This homily became a blend of Greek allegory and the exegesis of the rabbis. As we saw earlier, there has always been some dispute as to the early Christian indebtedness to the Hebrew roots. Some scholars wish to see the Christian gospel as discontinuous from the synagogue roots, while others see the roots. Some of those who see the roots see the Christian message as unique and the Christian age as inaugurating preaching as a new form of discourse. Thyen, rather, argues that it was the Jewish homily that was turned into the Christian sermon and uses Hebrews and the epistle of First Clement as examples of this indebtedness. In his view, the preaching of the synagogue prepared the way for Christian proclamation, and the Christian missionaries simply filled the Hellenistic synagogue forms with the cross.

Certainly Paul was influenced by Greek rhetoric. As an educated man he probably studied it as a discipline. His sermon on Mars Hill in Acts is a good example of a rhetorical discourse given Christian content. Thyen believes Paul's oral style was influenced by the Jewish Hellenistic homily. Since, he avers, Paul was a child of the Hellenistic synagogue and trained in its ways of preaching prior to his conversion, he really did not have to change form and style. Only the content was different.

Later, of course, and especially in the fourth century, the Christian leaders were trained rhetoricians and baptized their profane training with Christian faith. Even Origen was trained in Greek philosophy, as were the rhetoricians. If not trained in rhetoric itself, he certainly was a force in the history of Christian preaching, not only for his use of allegory (with both its strengths and weaknesses), but because the Cappadocians took Origen's influence and united it with their rhetorical training. When one looks at the fourth century, particularly in the East, Basil, Gregory of Nazianzus, Gregory of Nyssa, and John Chrysostom stand out. In the West, Ambrose and Augustine. All of these powerful leaders were trained in classical rhetoric—both Greek and Roman. The schools of rhetoric by this time were similar to liberal arts schools or colleges of humanities. It was broad-gauged training to fit students for a variety of fields of learning and occupation. Augustine's *Doctrine of Christianity*, Book 4, is in reality a baptism of Aristotle via Cicero. It is still a good example of a Christian rhetoric.[9]

It has been indicated earlier that Christian preaching cannot be allied completely with classical rhetoric. However, the reasons are not the ones usually given. Today we hear that rhetorical study is one of the problems responsible for the state of modern-day preaching and its malaise. Usually rhetoric is blamed for sterile outlines and structures, argumentation and proof as a sermon form, rationalistic discourse, set patterns, and propositional forms. Such a practice, if it has a heritage, can be attributed as much to scholasticism as to classical rhetoric. Indeed, early rhetoric could not be placed in a set pattern, as any reader of the earliest sermons knows. The real problem with classical rhetoric for Christian preaching is simply that Christian discourse does not fall into the categories of classical rhetoric. Even though some of the earliest Christian preachers attempted to adapt their rhetorical studies to the Christian gospel, they simply are not consonant. The traditional canons of speech communication which embrace the areas of *deliberative* (political, advisory), *forensic* (legal), and *epideictic* (ceremonial) speech, did not cover sufficiently the task of Christian preaching: neither its content (the gospel itself), nor its goal (calling for commitment). In spite of Thyen's comment about Paul, it is not only the content of the gospel, but the form and style, too, that are different for the Christian message.

It is for this reason that we look at the Christian gospel as the third strand in the history of proclamation. If the religion of the Old Testament and classical rhetoric provided two of the basic motifs for Christian preaching, it is the Christian gospel itself which became the capstone of proclamation for the Christian church. Some believe it was John the Baptist who was the connecting link between the Old and New Testaments. He was certainly in the prophetic tradition but was pointing to a new age. One way of considering his work is to see him as the last of a prophetic tradition and the first preacher of a new dispensation. His message indicates such an inauguration: "Repent, for the kingdom of heaven is at hand" (Matt. 3:2). These twin emphases were present in his preaching: inauguration of the kingdom and repentance.

The new kingdom was inaugurated by Jesus of Nazareth, according to John. For many, the Christian age of preaching began with Jesus and his preaching. His commission for that preaching comes from the passage from Isaiah which Jesus quotes as his mandate.

> The Spirit of the Lord is upon me,
> because he has annointed me to *preach* good news to the poor.
> He has sent me to *proclaim* release to the captives
> and recovering of sight to the blind,
> to set at liberty those who are oppressed,
> to *proclaim* the acceptable year of the Lord.
> (Luke 4:18–19, italics mine)

In spite of, or instead of, John the Baptist, Brilioth sees this commission of Jesus as the bridge between the Christian sermon and synagogue preaching. He goes further in seeing Jesus' commission taken from Isaiah as an emerging pattern which gives the key to the history of Christian preaching. For Brilioth[10] that pattern includes the *liturgical* (Jesus preaching in the context of the synagogue), the *exegetical* (exposition of the text from Isaiah), and the *prophetic* (divine authority which was much more than a textual commentator). Just as the preaching of the Jewish tradition gave us a suggestion of preaching content (i.e., what God has done, is doing, and will do), we now begin to see the development of *form* and *content* of the Christian sermon combined with the *role* or the authority of the preacher.

Brilioth's claims, while supportable on the surface and espoused by some, raise interesting questions. For one thing, can we assert unequivocally that the threefold pattern (liturgical, exegetical, prophetic) is normative for all preaching? The term "prophet," for example, as we have already seen in relation to priest, may not be as clear a model as is assumed. Apart from attempting to make the dichotomy between priest and prophet, there is the problem of the normal association of the prophetic only with the judgmatic. At the same time, the term does bring to the forefront the importance of the function or role of the preacher as well as the content. The foremost question, however, concerns Jesus himself as the paradigm for Christian preaching. It is assumed by many that his method of preaching not only was innovative in regard to the past but, in addition, also set the pattern for all Christian preachers, including the contemporary preacher. Those who make much of Jesus as the one preachers should emulate point to his use of parables, his commission (to which we have referred in the Lukan passage), and the message he preached as normative for all preaching.

It may not be as easy as we assume to talk about the preaching of Jesus, especially in regard to contemporary preaching. Even looking at the earthly life of Jesus and the gospel he preached presents problems. What was the content of his preaching? Was it the fulfillment of the kingdom of God, the kingdom of love, kingdom of heaven, or what? Are all of these the same, and what is the specific content? Even if we can delineate that message, we must ask if Jesus' preached message is enough for the abiding ages. Another difficulty is to square his preaching with the closing events of his life which are part and parcel of the Gospels. We then raise issues such as Jesus' messianic consciousness, the meaning of the cross, and the understanding of the resurrection faith. To use Jesus and his preaching as a model may make us ignore sections of the biblical records.

The critical factor in the development of early Christian preaching is that the preaching of Jesus and the preaching of the early church were not the same. The question is, can Jesus preach the gospel when he himself is part of it? As one scholar has said, though Jesus "came to preach the gospel, His chief object in coming was that there might be a gospel to preach."[11] Though it is true that the preaching of Jesus and that of the early church were not the same, it is unfair to claim they were totally different. In preaching, as in theology, we are tempted to make a dichotomy between Jesus of Nazareth and the Christ of faith.

Nevertheless, for the early church, the life, teaching, death, and resurrection of Jesus became the content of the preaching. While one would be cautious in going as far as Bultmann's statement that "theological thinking . . . begins with the *kerygma* of the earliest church and not before,"[12] yet there is undoubted truth to the claim that "the proclaimer became the proclaimed."[13] C. H. Dodd[14] elucidated *kerygma* as the kernel of New Testament preaching. That message was made up of the life, teaching, death, and resurrection of Jesus. He further pointed out that all other ethical instruction in the New Testament was not preaching but teaching. The pattern for the earliest preaching came specifically from Peter's sermons in Acts (2:14–36, 38–39; 3:12–26; 4:8–12). Dodd sees a pattern in these sermons which indicates the nature of the earliest preaching and notes that there have been those throughout history who also define preaching along the lines of this pattern.

1. Age of fulfillment has dawned. It is the messianic age prophesied by the prophets.
2. Messianic age takes place through the ministry, death, and resurrection of Jesus.
3. Jesus is exalted at the right hand of God.
4. Holy Spirit is in the church as a sign of the present power and glory.
5. Messianic age will reach consummation in Christ's return.
6. The gospel appeals for repentance, offers forgiveness, and promises salvation.[15]

It is obvious that this early church message, with the relegating of ethical instruction to another function of ministry, has implications for Christian faith as well as preaching in our day.

Dodd's thesis has been questioned and indeed refuted. Victor Furnish[16] and others have declared that the distinction between *kerygma* and *didache* is a false one. Ethical exhortation cannot be separated from the gospel proclamation; indeed, it is presupposed by and even identical with the *kerygma*. Also, *kerygma* is not synonymous with theological propositions or religious truths. It is not static. *Kerygma* is the activity of preaching and not simply a body of content to be transmitted. *Kerygma* is God's coming to humans in the preaching of the Word—not just the Word and its content. Weatherspoon[17] points out that there is no one Word for preaching in the New Testament, and it is therefore a mistake to limit the term to a narrow body of content.

The most serious objection to the split between *kerygma* and *didache* is that truncation of the gospel occurs. Without the proclamation of good news, preaching becomes only good advice. Without ethical instruction, preaching becomes irrelevant. Preaching in this case is *both/and*, not *either/or*. Early Christian preaching soon fostered different forms of preaching. While the earliest preaching may be what Dodd calls kerygmatic or missionary preaching, there came later post-baptismal preaching which was catechetical or instructional, and still later when the church had become more established, the homily for believers became part of the service of Eucharist.

In any event, though, the coming of Jesus, the formation of the Christian church, fused with classical rhetoric, and the worship inherited through the Jewish faith became the foundation for the Christian preaching tradition. The Old Testament *Heilsgeschichte* (what God has done, does, and will continue to do) joined with the prophetic authority of those who gave that message. Classical oratory provided an effective rhetoric for Christian proclamation, and the gospel itself provided the unique event which makes oratory Christian.

4

Words as a Medium of God's Presence

Criticism of preaching often comes from within the church itself and, strangely enough, from preachers. Often the charge is that pulpit proclamation is no longer viable communicatively. Though these charges appear from time to time, there is also a periodic renewal of preaching which counterbalances the criticisms. The interest in the pulpit comes from unexpected secular sources, as well as from within the church. In our time, especially, there is new interest in the Word, words, language, and speech. There are those who have either rediscovered the efficacy of the word, the foundational nature of human speech itself, and the importance of language; or, in most instances, who have never doubted those as being basic to communication among humans.

The preacher needs to consider the fundamental aspect of speech in human communication. For, in spite of the garbled rhetoric about the inadequacy of pulpit proclamation and the importance of the nonverbal, communication theorists are not confused as to the function of speech. Dr. Roy V. Wood, Dean of the Speech School, in a centennial address at Northwestern University, remarked that "Speech is the most special feature of the human being. The ability to symbolize and to process symbols is the characteristic that defines our humanity."[1] While smacking a recalcitrant plow horse across the head with a two-by-four may be a form of communication, human communication is of a different order. While we as humans can communicate on other levels, our unique capacity is the ability to elicit a response through verbal symbols.

Marshall McLuhan, of course, has been used by some to denigrate speech, and thereby preaching. Certainly his involving us in the electronic revolution has had tremendous impact on communication in our time. Yet, his work needs to be placed in perspective. His work has generated great interest, and many preachers have seemingly swallowed him hook, line, and thinker. A teaser and a prober, he is open to many kinds of interpretation and can be used for various purposes and in a variety of fields. The movement he represents needs to be taken seriously by those who preach. We must deal with McLuhan's concern neither by defensiveness out of fear nor by becoming McLuhaniacs out of faddism.

Although it is difficult to unpack all of McLuhan's many-sided claims,[2] one of the chief points is his belief that Gutenberg and the printing press are the culprits that took us from a preliterate oral society to a linear age in which literacy and typology locked us into a sequential, one-after-another word order which causes fragmentation and departmentalization. Above all, thinking and acting became separated from feeling and emotion. Now that the electronic revolution has come with television as the swashbuckling leader, we are in the new environment no longer with specialized segments but with Gestalt patterns signified by the global village concept. We have gone from content to total effect. The medium of communication is much more important than what is being communicated. Indeed, the form alters the content of communication. Television, for example, is altering our perception, not by what is shown but as a channel of mediating the message. There is an all-at-onceness in communication which no longer separates message from communication itself, which no longer fragments thought from feeling, which fosters unification and involvement, where events that occur to us are simultaneous happenings. Our perceptions and communications are multileveled and all-at-once as over against linear, sequential, fragmented, rationalistic, "hot." "Hot" is McLuhan's term for communication which is high in definition and low in participation. "Cool," by contrast, is that which is low in definition and is completed by our participation in the communicative process.

These brief teasers and probings have set religionists off with ammunition for criticizing preaching as being logical, linear, and analytical, while true communication is poetic, intuitive, and Gestalt. The pulpit monologue can no longer survive; we must find new forms which involve the congregation in participatory communication and which reach them through films, dance, and musical experiences that supplement, if not abolish, the spoken word. The nonverbal, nonrational aspects of communication simply cannot be transmitted by a person speaking to a group. Though there is no intention to give a full-blown criticism of his ideas, just as there has been no intent to give a full-blown treatment of his ideas, there are two observations that could be made in regard to the ideas raised by his rather unsystematic probings.

First, communication is certainly more than rational discourse. McLuhan is right to say that communication is more than meaning. A good sermon is an all-at-once communicative experience; it does transmit the nonverbal and the nonrational. It is—rightly conceived—a multileveled, existential discourse. Good preaching—like any good communication—would be a total communicative experience that entails complete involvement: an *event* relating God and people, people and people, preacher and God, people and preacher. An effective sermon should be effective communication. If preachers are not aware of preaching, then, we should not be surprised at those who go awhoring after other gods. To take only one example, if preachers scrounge around all week for exotic topics or general truths, structure those ideas, write and then read manuscripts verbatim, and label that "preaching," then it is no wonder that some are forsaking the pulpit as a lost cause.

Second, preachers have been too quick to accept the mythologies that have grown up around the McLuhan syndrome and have responded too rapidly with sweaty palms. The emphasis upon communication be- ing made today can be seen as an aid to the preaching enterprise. Take, for example, McLuhan's analysis of the periods from the tribal preliter- ate state through the Gutenberg literate stage to the present electronic age and the global village. His affirmation is that the electronic age is taking us once again into the realm of the total sensorium, and that the basic sensory experience is an oral one, as was the tribal society itself. Critics of McLuhan, as well as admirers, forget that he calls *speech* a "cool" medium. Of course, the various modes of speaking have higher and lower definitions and are therefore less "cool" or "hot," as the case may be. But speech itself—even in McLuhan's terms—is a "cool" medium. Words are media of speech, involving all the senses.

The McLuhan revolution, therefore, may not be as much of a threat as we think. For, on the one hand, it makes us aware that depth percep- tion of human communication is lacking in many preachers, and we have to share the responsibility for the one-dimensional speaking ema- nating from pulpits. On the other hand, the global village concept may lead us to a rediscovery of the spoken word as the primary vehicle for human communication.

While Dr. Frank Dance would agree with McLuhan that *print* is tied to the restrictions set by the Gutenberg revolution, *speech* is not. Indeed, he separates speech from writing and argues that *print* is the authority of monologue, while *speech* is dialogue. *Print* is alienation, *speech*, participation. *Print* encourages dependency, *speech* develops autonomy; *print*, sequentiality, *speech*, spontaneity.[3] Whether Dance is correct or not in his judgments on print, which are similar to McLuhan's criticisms, it is interesting to note this emphasis upon the basic function of the spoken word by a secular communicator at the very time religionists are unsure of its importance. Dance's theories lead to two other interesting observations about the function of human speech, especially as applied to preaching. There is a great deal of con- fusion between the nonverbal and the nonvocal. We hear a great deal about nonverbal forms of communication. "Nonverbal" has become a magical word like "communication" itself, particularly when used to signify the death of oral proclamation. Confusion is due to the fact that the uninitiated are using "nonverbal" when they mean "nonvocal." A verbal symbol can be either vocal or nonvocal, but all human communication is verbal. "A traffic signal derives its meaning from the observer's past experiences in learning law and order through words."[4] The traffic signal is nonvocal but verbal. Even deaf children communicate nonvocally, but their language is based upon words and the verbal. Helen Keller illustrates this point graphically in a moving passage from her autobiography. She had learned signs but not the meaning of language. She tells how she and her teacher went out to play and walked down to the well house. Her teacher placed her hand under the spout, and as the cool stream gushed over her hand, the teacher spelled into the other hand "water" over and over again. Somehow the mystery of language came to her. Says she:

> I knew then that w-a-t-e-r meant the wonderful cool something that was flowing over my hand. That living word awakened my soul, gave it light, hope, joy, set it free! . . . I left the well-house eager to learn. Everything had a name, and each name gave birth to a new thought. As we returned to the house every object which I touched seemed to quiver with life. That was because I saw everything with the strange new sight that had come to me.[5]

In somewhat the same vein, Brendan Gill, in a review of Marcel Marceau's performance in pantomime, asserts that "At the heart of pantomime is the sublimated anguish of lost speech."[6] He suggests that if there was not music accompanying the program, the audience might find the unspoken narratives unbearable.

These illustrations lead to the other point that Dance makes so tellingly: there is a distinction between *signs* and *symbols*. Signs are fixed, symbols are flexible; signs are often innate, symbols are always learned; signs are concrete, symbols are abstract; and, above all: "*all* symbols are verbal even though they may not be vocal."[7] A speaker once attempted to illustrate that the verbal was not needed (he really meant the vocal). His point evidently was designed to show the triumph of a sign (or symbol?) over the spoken word. He stated that if he sent his wife a dozen roses he was saying more than if he had sent an accompanying note or had said, "I love you." (This illustration raises interesting questions under the head of Everything-You've-Ever-Heard-About-Roses-and-Wives-and-Were-Afraid-to-Ask. A dozen roses at many houses might spell g-u-i-l-t as well as l-o-v-e.) The important point is that the speaker confused the verbal with the vocal. The flowers are a symbol of love, because they are based upon words stated beforehand and repeated again and again. The roses are a nice gesture, but unless they are based upon the words of love, they are a meaningless sign. Most wives would rather have the words than the flowers, for love will wilt, just as the flowers, if there are no words to express the love. "No sign can become a symbol except through the mediation of speech communication and language."[8] Hence the old saying that a picture is worth more than ten thousand words is "true only if the learning of the ten thousand words has preceded the viewing of the picture."[9]

Walter Ong is another communication theorist who affirms the spoken word as the central fact of human communication.[10] For Ong, a word is a spoken word even when written, for the word is an event in sound. It is the word which establishes contact with human existence. It is the primary medium of communication, for communication flowers in speech. Again, for Ong as for Dance, writing shifts the balance of sense from aural to visual. Words are living—not an inert record of meaning but something alive and active like sound. The human word exists in a mysterious connection with the divine. That is why for Ong, if not alone for theological reasons, the New Testament gospel (Word) is tied to the spoken word of humans. In the Old Testament, *dabar* in Hebrew ties together Word and Event. Apart from theology, however, verbal communication is a person's means of entering into the life and consciousness of others and thereby deeply into his own life.

Ong spells out his concern for the oral in much the same manner as McLuhan. In describing the stages of the word he, too, moves from the first stage (oral or oral-aural) to the second (script-alphabet-type) to the third (electronic). Rather than seeing the electronic age supplanting the oral, Ong contends that our oralism is lineally controlled as early oralism was not, but communication is still oral. Writing, for him, is derivative from speech, not *vice versa*. The sound of speech is a special sensory key to interiority, and the encounter between human and human is achieved largely through voice. It is sound that situates a person in the middle of actuality and in simultaneity, whereas vision situates us in front of things and in sequentiality. Further, thought itself is nestled in speech. Even deaf children, as we have seen, learn from vocalizers. They participate indirectly in a world held together by voices.

What we learn from these experts in communication theory, we find duplicated time after time in other fields. From Susanne Langer, who states, "The fact is that our primary world of reality *is* a verbal one,"[11] and Frank Dance, who defines human communication as one "eliciting of a response."[12] to Dr. Karl Menninger, who writes, "Talking it out, and being listened to, are a basic modality of human interrelation and not surprisingly, the medium of most psychiatric therapy,"[13] the evidence is the same. Ours is an oral culture, and humans communicate with one another verbally. A fascinating and provocative book by Paulo Freire, *The Pedagogy of the Oppressed*,[14] develops a teaching method of liberation or revolution based upon the importance of the word. In discussing dialogue as a human phenomenon, the author discovers that the essence of dialogue is the word. The word has two dimensions: action and reaction. Word has a praxis—action. Here is another example of those interested in endeavors touching upon human behavior defining communication as a spoken word in the basic human relationships, just at the moment some ministers may be feeling their greatest moments of doubt. As G. van der Leeuw has said:

> In this living speech . . . time becomes *kairos*, the "due *season*," *hic et nunc*. Whoever speaks, therefore, not only employs an expressive symbol but goes forth out of himself, and the word that he lets fall decides the matter. Even if I merely say "Good Morning" to someone I must emerge from my isolation, place myself before him and allow some proportion of my potency to pass over into his life, for good or evil.[15]

One of the mandates for the preacher is to capture again the magic of the spoken word—not to maintain the pulpit *status quo* defensively—but to give excitement once again to the preaching office.

If what is true about the spoken word finds its rootage in theories of speech communication and is corroborated in the other sciences of behavior, then it should come as no surprise that the importance of speech, word, and language should be at the heart of the religious experience of humans. Those who have worked in the phenomenology of religion have helped us see the place of the *word* in world religions, not alone Christianity. Scholars have written perceptively about the function of word in religious experience. Frederick J. Streng, for example, points out three aspects of the sacred Word: (1) it can have creative power; (2) it can serve as an intermediary by bearing within its form the absolute reality; and (3) it can reflect or point to an "other reality" that is the ground for, but essentially different from, the form that it takes. It is easy to see that such functions of word can be and are incorporated into the Christian gospel and even preaching itself. As Streng reminds us, "The Gospel (the good news) is the Sacred Word."[16]

The Word of God has always been thought of in some sacramental sense. Charles Winquist employs sacrament in the phenomenological sense in regard to Word. "The Word of God is the sacrament of the encounter with the reality of God."[17] Such a conclusion has a corollary insight that "the meaningful expression of a human intention toward another person requires an expressive word." What Winquist is affirming is simply what Streng and others have said, too, that the Word is "a modality for the manifestation of the sacred."[18] From this, then, it is easy to move to the concept of the Word creating the Event. Not alone through the affirmation we make about God creating through the Word, which is basic to the Word spoken, but through the use of language, *per se*, we see the creative act of making things come into being. It is Martin Heidegger who has claimed that "it is in words and language that things first come into being and are."[19] The intent of language is not simply to describe a situation but to transform one. Thus, Winquist can say that:

> The interpretation of the word of God is an *act* through which the sacred is made visible within the community. This is one of the reasons why we can properly talk about the sacrament of the word of God. Speaking and hearing the word of God lies beneath the sacramental activity of the church and it is itself a modality for the continuing presence of the revelation of God.[20]

If word, language, and human speech are all basic elements in human relationships, and if the same phenomena are carried over into our communication with the Divine, we should be clear, then, about the genesis of God's self-revelation. For the Christian this revelation is in the natural world through the creative Word, in Jesus Christ the Logos, and in the Scriptures which bear our salvation history and become again our present history. And, finally, in the words of the faithful preacher who represents for our time this story of God's coming to us and creates thereby an event in which lives are changed as they participate in this drama of the gospel enacted before their very eyes in speech. It is no wonder, then, that we can affirm that the Word and the

Event are not alone the province of a specific brand of Protestant theology.

William L. Malcomson's *The Preaching Event*[21] is poles apart from the biblical, theological, Word-Event school as it is usually thought of. Malcomson believes that preaching is an event because it is situational or contextual. He means that preaching is meeting people's needs. We preach to people by aiming at their depths and by throwing the light of the gospel on those human needs. The thrust of Malcomson's book is focused on the human level, and the theology expressed—or rather unexpressed—fits the framework of helping humans. To delineate the preaching event, he isolates such things as the sermon, the preacher, the congregation, the worship service, the physical situation, and the community.

However, it is usually when the work of certain biblical and/or theological scholars is discussed that the term Word-Event has its most popular currency. Though the discussion is usually in terms of basic theological or biblical studies, it would be incorrect to overlook the concern for preaching which is involved in these studies—first, last, and always. One example of the concern for preaching, and the basis upon which many have structured their work in the field of homiletics, has been the Word-Event theology clustered around the work of Ernst Fuchs and Gerhard Ebeling. There is no need to detail the essence of their positions, but they do exhibit the fact that the Reformation doctrine of the preached word being vitally related to the Word of God is still a viable view.

As Ebeling understands it, the word of God enters language, though the event it creates and to which it refers is more than mere speech. It has to do with reality which it changes, for the conception of word entails an encounter. Ebeling sees the Word-Event as communication, since the words which take place make partners and participation. "Language opens up the space to us in which the event of the word can take place."[22] The words uttered effect something and are not alone carriers of meaning. Because we are addressed by God, we speak. Thus, the event of the Word of God is bound up with the life of language itself. The Word of God becomes proclamation, because we are addressed in present-day language, and when the proclamation of what the text has proclaimed becomes proclamation again in present experience, then the Word has been spoken and the Word has created the Event for the hearer—who is really a participant. The Word, rightly viewed, is an Event like love—which involves at least two people. The structure of Word is not statement, which is an abstraction of the Word-Event, but appraisal, not in the sense of information, but in the fuller sense of participation and communication. When Word rightly occurs, existence is illumined. The preacher imparts himself or herself to the other and opens the hearer's future by awakening faith within. To sum up Ebeling's thought—along with a host of others including the essential Reformation view itself—we hear these words:

> It is the Reformation insight that faith comes from the spoken word, that is, that the message—though certainly coming from the Bible and drawing from its text and confirmed by its text—is handed on from man to man, from nation to nation by word of mouth, one might even say, personally, not anonymously, in such a way that the witness is entirely exposed and ready for the utmost surrender. He is not like a postman, who just delivers letters whose contents he does not know; nor like a herald, who ceremoniously reads out a proclamation; but he is like a responsible deputy who has been given full powers to speak. If the word of faith—which the New Testament calls the gospel—had not reached us in this way, by word of mouth, by being passed on personally, then we should know nothing about faith.[23]

After hearing these words, is it any wonder John McKenzie says that preaching is ineffective because we do not believe in the power of the Word? That is why preachers are frightened, says he. They are afraid of the power of the Word—that something might happen.[24]

Though Ebeling's view is by no means normative for biblical scholars or theologians, it is an example of the thinking associated with Word-Event theology. Another writer might be mentioned in regard to Word-Event theology. Peter Hodgson makes the point strongly that if God is present to all, it is by means of Word. In his discussion of the death-of-God theologians, he affirms that if God seems to be absent or dead, it is only because God is present by means of words, and they are finite, fragile, and susceptible of failure. His main thesis is that word is the medium of presence. In the process of speaking, humans are gathered into presence in both a temporal and a spatial sense. The spoken word is the primordial form. God's power is designated as God's

Word, precisely because its essence is that it be spoken—it happens as a temporal event calling forth our existence. It does not exist as an eternal truth. We are not communicating or transmitting objective content, as though the purpose of word were statement or assertion. Rather, the communication is an event, an encounter.

Yet the experience transmitted by the word which produces an event and an encounter is not devoid of meaning. While it is not propositional truth, it is meaningful. It is at this point that Amos Wilder is most critical of the Word-Event theology of Fuchs and Ebeling. While agreeing with the emphasis upon the Word as human word, Wilder insists upon the Word as meaning. He does not want the Word to be simply an existential category, but Word which addresses man and woman as cultural beings. He resists seeing the divine Word and the human response in a kind of cultural vacuum. He is nervous about revelation which is unrelated to meaning. Our will is not enough in response; reason and imagination must be accounted for. The Word of God has structure. For him, the Word has a meaningful content. The faith response is not only voluntaristic, it is also noetic. "Faith involves consent to truth as well as obedience to an invitation or a call."[25] Wilder makes the same point made earlier in this chapter that word and speech upon which Word-theology is based is a phenomenon related to anthropology, linguistics, and other social sciences. While my use of materials from these fields was the basis for theology and preaching—based on word as the primordial means of communication—Wilder uses the same data to remind the theologians that the cognitive element in speech, gesture, and language would have to be taken seriously.

What we have seen, then, is that the spoken word is the basic means of human communication in the cultural, as well as the theological, sense. Speech communication theorists, language specialists, and social scientists have all affirmed the primary function of the verbal in human communication. This insight, buttressed by the phenomenologists of religion, is the obvious foundation for a theology that presumes that God speaks to us through the medium of human words. Though theologians may not all be interested in the specific cultural background of the spoken word, it is just as real as their premise of the Word being a function of God's revelation. The theological and the cultural belong together. The *Word* is not verbal Gnosticism. Ours is an incarnational religion, and the Word that became flesh and spoke through the prophets and speaks through his messengers is a human word in a historical setting. The Word of faith and the words of humans in our cultural climate are of the same order.

Another insight—equally important—is that the Word has meaning. The event which the Word creates is not a subjective happening devoid of structure and understanding. Meaning is not limited to the noetic or the cognitive, but it certainly includes them. Meaning is of the emotions, will, and the existential self, but the event cannot be free from interpretation and even structure, if it is to communicate itself to people and from one to another. This point makes its presence felt when, in an endeavor to get away from the heavy-handed structure and rationalistic discourse of a wooden pulpiteer, we want to sweep away all verbal interpretation and turn the worship experience into a giant "happening" rife with subjectivism. Occasions devoid of meaning are just that—subjective happenings devoid of meaning. The Christian experience is not designed for emotional catharsis of aesthetic appreciation or for that which makes us feel "good" or "happy." Our kind of religious experience is logos-worship born out of a God who is revealed in a meaningful way, meeting us in an encounter that demands obedience and righteous living. The verbal symbol is a basic human communicative instrument, because it conveys meaning.

With all of these supporting views of the efficacy of the word, it is easy to see what was alluded to earlier: many critics are tilting at the wrong windmills. They continue to lambast preaching, when their real quarrel is with communication theorists and theologians. The relationship between preaching and theology has been going on for some time. The homiletician and the theologian have often lodged in the same house—even the same body. H. H. Farmer, to name only one, saw the theologian and the preacher linked. He also added Buber's insight of I-Thou to the preacher's understanding. The "necessity of preaching resides in the fact that when God saves a man through Christ He insists on a living, personal encounter with him here and now in the sphere of personal relationships."[26] This is obviously not preaching that sends monologic thunderbolts hurling from pulpits onto the heads of believers and unbelievers alike. It is seeing Christian preaching in the context of understanding persons and their relationships with one another. The I-Thou concept is essential to preaching, and speech is absolutely indispensable in the world of personal relationships. For the spoken word is right within the core of the I-Thou relationship.

Farmer makes an interesting threefold case for the necessity of speech in human relationships, and hence, in preaching. (1) The *will*. The essence of personal relationship is not in the activity of my will but the activity of your will when you encounter me and bring the word into being. (2) Speech is also packed with *claim*. When one speaks, a claim is laid on the other. (3) Speech conveys *meaning* and *understanding*. Music evokes feeling, or art an aesthetic impact, or gesture a suggestion. "The unique function of speech is that of conveying in the most explicit way possible the judgment of one self-conscious awareness to another in such wise that both are brought directly and inescapably under the claim of truth."[27]

A more contemporary writer, Kyle Haselden,[28] likewise insists upon the primacy of the spoken word in extolling the role of preaching. He thinks that the ebbing of the power and compulsion of preaching can be traced to the clergy's loss of confidence in the power of the spoken word. Yet to him, a journalist as much as a preacher, the spoken word is the best weapon—the superlative tool in the communication of the gospel, superior to all other forms of communication. This superiority is due to the fact that it is an instrument especially suited to the promulgation of a gospel; it is the form into which an urgent message most naturally flows.

Though we are dealing primarily with the crisis of the modern preacher and trying to demonstrate the efficacy of the spoken word both as a phenomenon of human communication and as a theological act, we cannot entirely overlook the specific preparation of the sermon. It should be obvious that a view which couples revelation with human speech and God's Word with the spoken word does not take the job of climbing into the pulpit each Sunday lightly. Yet the agony has its counterpart in ecstasy, though the latter is unpredictable. It is only accepted with thanks when it appears as grace. For the sermon becomes God's words, not through the preacher's own manipulation but when through God's grace they are made so in the encounter and Event which occurs when the Word is spoken. For as Paul Holmer reminds us, preaching is first and foremost one way to be faithful. To the Christian, this means telling the story through words.

In spite of the critics, then, it seems established that the spoken *word* is the instrument of human communication. And it is the word in its theological usage, which, coupled with the factor of human speech, evolves in the preaching of the gospel. And, despite the preacher's own dispiritedness, there are signs that the preaching office is undergoing renewal and is even flowering in some quarters in Christendom.

One is reminded of the scene in Archibald MacLeish's drama *J.B.*, where a group of people are huddled together after a holocaust. A mother and child clinging together speak:

Jolly Adams: *screaming*
                               Mother! Mother! What was
                      That?
Mrs. Adams: The wind, child. Only the wind.
                      Only the wind.
Jolly Adams: I heard a word.
Mrs. Adams: You heard the thunder in the wind.
Jolly Adams: *drowsy*
                      Under the wind there was a word—[29]

Yes, in the wind there was a Word, and that Word brings one freedom, love, grace.

5

Using the Bible
Biblically

Assuming the authority of the Bible for the Christian community and the place of the lectionary in one's yearly preaching, how does the sermon develop? Here again, it is difficult to be dogmatic. One can state general principles for all preachers, but sermons are individual creations. The key question in biblical preaching is how one moves from text to sermon. The preacher stands in two worlds, metaphorically speaking, and the task is to bridge those two spheres of Bible (tradition, theology, church) and the world (culture, people, parish). When the preacher goes into the study, the task becomes that of bringing those two worlds together. Karl Barth is reported to have said that the preacher holds the Bible in one hand and the newspaper in the other. It is in the tension between these poles that creative sermons are born. In terms of the development of the biblical sermon one of the simplest things to say is that a genius can do it without much agony, while the rest of us who preach simply struggle and hope for the best.

As we saw in regard to the lectionary, the preacher with the lessons at hand every week makes a natural progression to the sermon issuing from those texts. One of the best reminders is to combine the devotional study of the lessons with sermon preparation. Before "jumping" to the sermon idea, the preacher lives with the texts, reads them over time after time, and becomes immersed in the week's readings. The process of "getting started" is also enhanced by reading the different versions. Though some preachers seem to be locked into one version or another, often born out of theological commitment, there is no reason why the preacher should not read the lessons for the coming Sunday in a variety of versions. The variation of style and word choice can emit new meanings and fresh insights that enrich the preacher's thought. This is particularly important for those who are not at home in the original languages of the Bible. The various versions can compensate for lack of linguistic skills and can give broader insights into a passage.

Living with the text through the early part of the creative process is more than reading the passages and making comparisons with a variety of versions. The wise preacher will be taking notes and writing down the insights that come as he or she reads and absorbs. Many ideas may seem farfetched and may be unusable, but jotting down even fleeting insights is a way of capturing ideas that should be preserved. In a way, this process is almost a stream of consciousness act, recording those bits and pieces which come into our mind's eye. If one can resist the temptation of looking for the sermon, making an outline, or searching for the clever title, the process of reading and brooding over the material may be the most valuable aspect of the entire act of sermonizing. This will be true, especially if the preacher has garnered many notes that will be grist for the mill when the sermon goes through the steps of refinement. This first step might very well be called an impressionistic understanding of the text.

Though this impressionistic step is important, a good many other things may also be occurring when one is dealing with the text. One may be a dialogue with the passage, a struggle, or a wrestling, a kind of personal encounter that issues forth even in quarreling with the passage, as the preacher works with the material. That may be the most painful and rewarding of all experiences. Another preacher will consider the time with the lessons a personal meditation or spiritual brooding over the text. Still others will see the time spent with the text as an existential understanding of the Scripture, letting it speak in a personal way before it becomes personal word and history for the congregation. Whatever the methodology, whatever the process is labeled, the time spent in the early stages of sermon development with the text itself, recording impressions, feelings, meanings, and even one's own reactions to the Scripture, is not meaningless. It is the essence of the creative process which, of course, would be true of other artistic endeavors as well. What we have called the *impressionistic paraphrase* (whether written out or not) is perhaps an indispensable step in the preaching process and should not be short-circuited too quickly by rushing to the commentaries, before the preacher has gone through his or her own reactions to the pericope.

The next step—also an indispensable one—is the exegesis of the passage. There is the temptation of bypassing this step or of going to it too early and leaving it too soon. Many sermons are really only the impressions of the preacher as to what the passage is all about. They may be interesting and even helpful, yet not have come to terms with the meaning of the text. Exegesis seems to frighten a good many preachers. Most of us have in one way or another learned the tools of exegesis in seminaries, yet we have trouble transferring that knowledge into the sermon. It should be clear that a sermon is more than a wooden exegesis of a passage. Much of the work of the study should not come out in the sermon. Further, exegesis should not suggest that we come to a passage *de novo*. We come to the commentaries and the Scripture with our own ideas, the needs of the parish, the concerns of the world, and our own interests and biases *(eisegesis)*. The exegesis, which includes commentaries, does not address a passive nonentity. At the same time, exegesis is an indispensable step for the minister who seeks to be a faithful expositor of the Scriptures.

The steps in exegesis vary, but the analysis of the passage is necessary. This process involves individual word study, grammar of the sentence structure, the context in which the passage is situated, the historical background, the author and book of which it is a part, and the total biblical viewpoint. Though such analysis will not come out in the sermon, it reveals imperative data for the preacher before the sermon gets too far along. In addition, one gets beyond the Bible itself by asking theological questions of the text and the meaning of the text in light of the witness and affirmations of the church. The study of a specific passage is somewhat like dropping a stone in the midst of a quiet pond and having the waves go concentrically until they touch the contemporary shore. The study does not need to be ominous, even for those who feel bereft without the tools. Such study can be thought of as simply answering the questions, what does the text say? and what does it mean? what does it say about the human situation? what does it say about God? how do I react to it? There are innumerable books on biblical preaching which give help in exegesis, particularly in its relationship to the sermon.[1]

The major question for the preacher, however, is, how does all of this material become a sermon? Perhaps one of the unfortunate aspects of preaching is that we have tended to separate the exegesis from the other parts of the sermonic process, as if we have the Bible out of the way and now on to the sermon. Lloyd Bailey states that, "Some authors define 'hermeneutic' as the overall process of interpretation (of which 'exegesis' is the initial step), while others view the hermeneutic problem as emerging only after the exegesis is finished."[2] The preacher would be helped greatly if he or she thought of the entire process as hermeneutics, so that the process of interpretation would be in the mind from the beginning and would keep the exegetical step from being simply exercise. If the preacher's creation is only an exegetical exercise, then it is not a sermon. "The movement from exegesis (what the text said to its own time) to application (what the text *says;* its implications for the 'believing community' in the present) transforms a lecture into a sermon."[3] The preacher's key role is to bring alive sermonically what has been going on in the study.

Moving from the study into the pulpit is the crucial step in preaching, the one where the sermon usually succeeds or fails, and the time which one might call the agony and ecstasy of preaching. It is the time when the most creative preachers among us seem to have the easiest time and the rest of us the greatest struggle. Some preachers are more creative than others. They seem to have a penchant for the artistic or minds that are more "homiletically" inclined. Some also have better intellects than others. To assume preaching is not a kind of an intellectual endeavor is to denigrate both the preaching act and the gospel itself. Some preachers reach into a pile of accumulated material and pull out a handful of "nothing," or at best a "fist" full of cliches. Others reach in and come out with arresting and creative sermon ideas.

Those who were called into the ministry, however, are not called because of academic prowess, intellectual superiority, or skill in creative thinking. Although all of these are important for the preacher, most ministers, through diligent effort, can take raw material and work it through until it becomes a faithful sermon. One way, of course, is to ask questions of the material: what is there in this passage (or assembled material) that stands out for me? how does this Scripture address the needs of my people? how can I make this ancient word "come alive" in our day? of what issues in our time does this material remind me? Questions such as these can begin to focus the material into a manageable sermon idea.

Another fruitful concept is the development of an *interpretive*[4] *paraphrase*. Earlier we suggested that after the preacher has initially been immersed in the Scripture on his or her own, what usually emerges from those early stages could be called an *impressionistic paraphrase*, if it were written out in essay form. After one has gone through this first step of familiarizing oneself with the body of Scripture, and then moved to the exegesis (commentaries, dictionaries, etc.), there appears a different dimension. Earlier impressions may have to be discarded: new insights have come. Earlier views need to be revised, and the preacher now encompasses both the personal dimension so necessary to the sermon and the solid biblical study so indispensable to preaching. At this point, if the preacher sits down with the biblical text and paraphrases the passage in his or her own words, verse by verse, in light of the original personal reactions and the scholarship on the text that was done subsequently, what results will be an *interpretive paraphrase*.

The *interpretive paraphrase* written out can do several things. First, it will be a capsule of the Scripture as it is seen at this point of time, filtered through the preacher, and related to the congregation. Second, it will be the bridge between the exegesis of the sermon and the sermon itself—the very place most preachers have a great deal of problems, and where sermons seem split in two between the study and the pulpit. Third, and perhaps most importantly, by the time the paraphrase is finished, the preacher will be able to formulate clearly the central idea of the sermon. That central idea, or the main affirmation, of the sermon makes the unfolding of the sermon possible. That main affirmation can be called the *thesis* of the sermon.

Surprisingly, there is a great deal of negative reaction to the idea that a sermon should have a clear, main idea that controls the sermon. Some suggest that we live in a frenetic, kaleidescopic world where persons do not think logically, and we apprehend material holistically through an all-at-onceness. The age of McLuhan and TV convinces some that parable, indirect discourse, pictorial narrative, etc., are ways to unfold the gospel message. Besides, that kind of an approach leaves room both for the imaginative unfolding of a message and the comprehension of it by the listeners. To these persons, a thesis suggests a rationalistic discourse, defending the proposition as in a debate, a lawyer's brief transferred to the pulpit, argumentation, scholastic outlines, and sterile rhetoric. Such presentations avoid the affective level and tend to transfer ideas from minds to minds.

Yet, many sermons fail, simply because they are not clear. Preachers will raise several ideas in the beginning of a sermon and either develop one, or several, or none. People do not know what it is all about, and it becomes a mystery hour. What some take for creativity and expressive language may in reality be evidence of a fuzzy mind. Private parables in the name of self-expression and empathetic or indirect discourse, can lead to purposeless meanderings. Whatever else the gospel is, it is at least meaningful. Surely it is much more than cognition and does reach the affective level. It is a holistic event which combines mind, heart, emotions, and physical presence. At the core, however, is the preacher's concern to unfold the claims of the gospel meaningfully. Fred Craddock, in his book, *As One Without Authority*, makes critical comments about sermons which are "impaled upon the frame of Aristotelian logic," and have "monotonous method of outlining." Nevertheless, in calling for the necessity of the unity of the sermon, he says, "The desired unity has been gained when the preacher can state his central germinal idea in one simple affirmative sentence."[5]

A central germinal idea which is clear in the preacher's mind— even if not stated boldly in the sermon—goes a long way to insure both the clarity and the unity of the sermon. This thesis is not a proposition to be proved but is the unifying magnet goal toward which the sermon moves. It is most effective when it is a simple declarative sentence. If it takes two or three sentences or a paragraph to state the thesis, then that may be a sign that the sermon is covering too much. An abundance of dashes, semicolons, parentheses, modifying phrases, and complex or compound sentence structures in the thesis may indicate a complex idea or a lack of precision on the part of the preacher. The one simple, declarative sentence focuses both the mind of the preacher and the listener—even if it is never stated as such in the sermon.

As a one-sentence statement, the thesis should have a strong predicate as well as a subject. A predicate will indicate an action step that gives a sermon legs and sometimes wings. An intransitive verb also will weaken a thesis. "God is love" is a nice sentiment, but as the thesis for a sermon it raises the question, "So what?" "The power of prayer" without verb or a predicate is a theme or a title but not a thesis. The predicate also helps to answer that other embarrassing homiletical question, "How to?" A better approach to the above examples would be "God's love calls us to . . ." or "the power of prayer enables the Christian to . . .". Normally the thesis is not a question. To answer a question which is not an affirmation gets one into a debate motif or an argumentative stance.

The key test for the thesis, however, is the preacher's ability to state the sentence without resorting to biblical or theological language—jargon. Can one, without psychologizing the gospel or going through the process of theological reductionism, state the thesis in his or her own words? To eliminate the jargon or pious language and yet make an affirmative statement about the Christian gospel is the challenge for the preacher in our time. To have a thesis such as, "In Christ's sacrificial death, we have been brought to new life," may have meaning to the preacher, but unless stated in words that push beyond the language, chances of appropriation on the part of the listener are slim. Further, the rhetoric of the sermon will be of the same order. That kind of pious affirmation in a sermon may ring some emotional bells to those who bring a background consonant with the piety of traditional language but will hardly suffice to address the majority of our age. At the same time, the preacher's ability to put the old wine of traditional theological language into the new wine skins of the language of our day may be the greatest challenge and the most rewarding aspect of the modern-day pulpit.

Bridging the gap between the Bible and the sermon can be exciting when one takes the Scripture seriously and is determined to make its truths come alive in our day. Personal confrontation with the Bible by the preacher, coupled with serious study, can make its Word become Word for the preacher. Stating it in his or her own words, as we say in the *interpretive paraphrase*, and then formulating a thesis for the sermon will lead the material to its expression as a sermon for others. The hermeneutical process that begins with the study and exegesis of the text and moves through a paraphrase and a thesis, is ready for the sermon's development—whatever the form.

6

From Study
to Sermon

Many sermons are like the universe before creation. They are without form and void. Yet, there is resistance to outline and structure for the same reasons that there is objection to formulating a thesis. To some, structure smacks of rationalistic propositions, proofs, argumentation, wooden sermons, and sterile preaching. Often such preaching is characterized humorously as three points, a poem, and a prayer. Though criticisms such as these are often given by responsible persons, it is really difficult to find a teacher of homiletics who purports to teach such methods. Other than printed "sermon helps" or "ministers' manuals," it is almost impossible to find much data to support the contention that preachers are being taught to devise argumentative and wooden outlines.

Some of the more serious critics, however, are teachers of homiletics who, for a variety of reasons, are skeptical of outlines and structures. There are those who contend that classical rhetoric is the culprit. As we saw earlier, classical rhetoric is a complex subject, and Scholasticism (both Protestant and Roman) probably had more affect on outlining, sub-dividing, and argumentation than did early Greek or Roman rhetoric. Other critics are persuaded that preaching is an art form where narrative, story, parable, and pictures are the ways persons respond to oral presentations and that outlining or structure is neither necessary nor compatible with these approaches. Part of this view is a concern for holistic communication, and some is due to the feeling that since persons do not think sequentially but pictorially, sermon methodology must change to reach persons in this new communicative age. Obviously there is much truth here, even though such points of view often recruit fuzzy-headed and lazy preachers who embrace such ideas with alacrity.

Linear thinking and development do have grave limitations. Even before McLuhan we have known that. The movement in drama called the "Theater of the Absurd" has shown incisively the unreality of believing that life is logical and that persons themselves are rational beings. Martin Esslin[1] points out that the premises of the traditional theater have gone. There is no accepted moral order, belief in automatic progress is no longer viable, and right or wrong are no longer clear categories. Coupled with these are the decline of religious faith, the discovery of irrational and unconscious forces within the psyche, and the development of totalitarianism and mass destruction. For Esslin, if we live in a world without faith, meaning, and genuine freedom, then the theater of the absurd is the true theater of our age. To the extent that Esslin is right, then, we can see parallels to communicating, not only with persons who sit at the plays but also with those of this age who sit in the pews.

To keep the theater analogy, a more recent statement by Roger Copeland[2] reflects another point of view. He agrees that there are filmmakers and playwrights who reflect in their work that life is not well made, that life does not always follow sequentially, and that events do not always have beginnings, middles, and ends. Nevertheless, he is not sure that exhausts all there is to say about either life or the theater. While we may have lost faith in linear orderliness, some of the most moving and lasting plays of our time are structured in this seemingly outmoded manner. He cites Eugene O'Neill's *Long Day's Journey into Night* and even Edward Albee's *Who's Afraid of Virginia Woolf* as examples of time-honored principles of dramatic construction, developing in a linear fashion and concentrating on a single action in a so-called claustrophobic setting. His point is that

despite the fact that words like "linear" and "Aristotelian" have taken on pejorative and unfashionable connotations, a distinctive theatrical power still resides there, waiting to be tapped like so much fissionable material approaching critical mass.[3]

To make this point, he illustrates with the play *Night, Mother*, by Marsha Norman, which recently won a Pulitzer Prize. While acknowledging that many of our best current playwrights do use nonlinear devices, he makes a telling point that

in the hands of lesser dramatists, non-linear often means nondemanding, a surrender to the lazy perceptual habits of people raised on television. . . . In this country—at this point of time—the truly radical, challenging dramas may well be those that proceed in a linear fashion.[4]

The comparison to preaching may be drawn without forcing the analogy. We do live in a world where innovation is called for, and free-form may be a way of communicating through oral discourse. For those who have problems with the terms "outlines" and "structures," it might be well to think in other categories. It can be as simple as Aristotle's beginning, middle, and end. An old story tells of a young ministerial student, who complained that a bird flew through the church window, and the congregation began watching the bird rather than listening to the sermon. A professor to whom he was speaking observed that, "Perhaps the bird was moving and the sermon was not." Regardless of the content or form of a sermon, there should be movement and progression. One cannot hold attention with either circular development or no development. In the first instance, it is like a moth going around a light bulb until finally—"Pfft"—it is gone. In the second case, the sermon sits down like a baked apple right on the pulpit.

Whatever form the sermon takes, then, it needs movement and progression. Whether parable, story, pastoral, controversial, textual, or whatever method of procedure or type, an effective sermon takes some shape. It is for this reason that the preacher needs to be concerned with the central affirmation or thesis and the form that the sermon will take. Whatever the superstructure of rhetoric—whether written or oral—the underpinnings will need to be clearly thought through, not only to insure clarity, but also like any art form, to take a shape that allows the sermon to unfold with arresting movement. The structure, outline, shape, or form need not stand out in the sermon, though it should be pointed out that overclarification is not one of the gravest faults of modern preaching. However, the basic movement of the sermon should be crystal clear to the preacher before he or she leaves the study and before it is written or verbalized.

Some preachers and students affirm that they must write as their first step. Some say that they think better with a pen in hand or that they must write an introduction to get started. For some, writing a manuscript is the way a sermon unfolds. Accomplished persons who are writers often resist structure. There are, of course, many methods, and no one suffices for all. At the same time, there are those who make these arguments, who have trouble in thinking through an idea clearly. For them, it is easier to write than face the difficult task of wrestling with the theme in order to structure it. In addition, many inveterate writers end up wedded to their rhetoric and are obliged to take their manuscripts into the pulpit and virtually read them to their congregations. The point here is not the importance of writing. Writing should be done by every thoughtful preacher. The only question is where it should come in the sermonic process. The contention here is that for most preachers the writing should come after the ideas have been thought through carefully. In fact, many effective preachers write their sermons only after they deliver them in order to keep the spontaneity of oral communication with their congregations.

To refute those who affirm that an outline will be cumbersome, detailed, and much like a lawyer's brief, as if one were proving a proposition, the structure should be relatively simple. Though we are not discussing delivery at this point, it is well to note that a detailed outline as well as a manuscript can get in the way of effective communication of the sermon. Simplicity is as effective for preaching as it is for acting, painting, music, or any other art form. Some tend to believe that profundity goes hand-in-hand with complexity. Rather, complexity often means confusion, and simplicity in no way should connote simple-mindedness.

A simple outline that shows movement, presupposes a simply stated thesis, and is readily visible—at least to the preacher—will not only help him or her keep a grasp on the subject but will also enable the congregation to follow the movement of the sermon. Without reviewing in detail college freshman English, where undoubtedly one learned something about "outlining," and perhaps had more of that than one wished, there is something that we may remember from some dark and distant past. In studying theme writing some of us were reminded of three old chestnuts, *unity-coherence-emphasis*. While not as important a triumvirate as St. Paul's faith, hope, and love, they do have merit as a rationale for a sermon outline or structure. *Unity* is provided if the preacher has a well-worded thesis. *Coherence* simply indicates the flow of the sermon. Transition sentences are like bridges which get us from one point to another. Some sermons sound as if the bridge has washed out, and the preacher finishes one section of a sermon and moves to another as if it is a different sermon, with no connection between what has gone before or what is coming after. Transitions provide the coherence which insures movement and flow. *Emphasis* is the time spent in one place or another in a sermon. This is not clock time, of course, but indicates the emphasis the preacher is giving to the variety of material in the sermon. For example, many preachers tend to have long introductions, overlong analysis of this or that, and then too brief a time in affirming the gospel or solving the problem they themselves have introduced. It is easier always to diagnose than to prescribe, to be critical rather than to be positive, and to analyze rather than to construct; but in the study, at least, the preacher can see from an outline where the time is spent and what is important in terms of content and delivery.

We need to see that outlines or structures are not alone cognitive or rational entities. They also serve psychological and persuasive functions. For example, one way to think of a sermon structure is to think of the movement of the congregation's attention from the beginning to the climax. The outline usually gives the preacher a chance to see if the questions of "How to?" or "So what?" have been answered. At the same time, the outline will enable the preacher to see if there are emotional climaxes as well as logical ones. In short, a structure is not primarily for the congregation—except derivatively. In the first and primary instance, it is for the preacher, in order to have a clear grasp of the sermon before leaving the study. This will be prior to manuscript, speech notes, or the verbalized sermon.

Assuming that biblical preaching is the normative stance for the preacher, and that the lectionary has provided the starting place, the forms for unfolding the sermon are limitless. One's own creativity can be given free rein in developing the sermon. Plumbing the depths of a parable, a story, an incident, or even an entire book like Jonah or Philemon may lead one to such a simple development as telling or re-telling the story in one's own words, stating what it means, and applying it to our lives. Whether done in three points, one point, or two points is not the decisive thing in developing the sermon. Such simplicity leads one to movement and flow, which is the key factor in structure.

One might take a passage of Scripture, such as Isaiah's experience in the Temple (Isa. 6:1–8). Willard L. Sperry[5] years ago suggested that experience as a pattern of worship. Vision—Confession—Redemption—Dedication are easily discernible as the passage is read. Though the points made are Sperry's, they obviously come from the pericope. Such a classical pattern has also served as a sermon outline on the theme of the "movement of worship." If the preacher treats each point in a then (Isaiah) and now (us) sequence, the sermon gets the congregation involved quickly in the message, without waiting until the latter stages of the sermon, as many preachers do. Often the sermon suggests that the Scripture has been disposed of and now we can go on to a sermon.

Another example of the form a sermon might take comes from a sermon entitled, "Amos and the Sins of Civilization," based upon Amos 6:1–7. The preacher made the following three points from that passage: (1) national pride, (2) moral corruption, and (3) falseness of religion. The points were his, but the key element is that they were derived exegetically from the passage. This illustration, as the one from Sperry, simply suggests that a passage or pericope lends itself to a variety of forms and patterns, limited only by the creativity of the preacher.

Often, an effective sermon develops by simply walking the congregation through a passage, making adaptations and allusions as one goes. A distinguished New Testament scholar and former colleague, the late Dr. Kendrick Grobel, was a master of this method.[6] Dr. Fred Craddock has the same ability, often taking a passage and journeying through the Scripture in a most arresting way, stating it in his own words and making allusions—almost asides and often humorous—to our situation. Though there is a temptation to "stringiness" in the hands of less gifted preachers, there is much to be said for this modern expository mode of preaching.

Many teachers, in categorizing sermons, have made distinctions between expository and textual preaching in regard to biblical material used in the pulpit. By such definitions the foregoing examples would be expository and the next ones would be textual. However, since we do not preach definitions but sermons, the distinctions are not that significant. Usually, an expository sermon is simply a sermon that deals with a larger segment of biblical material than a textual one does.

The most obvious form of a textual sermon occurs when the preacher extracts a single text from a passage of Scripture as the basis of the sermon. In former times and in some older books on preaching, textual preaching was even defined as a sermon in which the structure is furnished by the structure of the text. Such a definition would lead to a wooden interpretation of the text and a resultant wooden sermon. In some obvious texts as, "Jesus said, 'I am the Way, the Truth, and the Life' " such a prescription might work, but it would be stretching the exegesis to assume every text lent itself to such homiletical treatment. The fact is that the test of a biblical sermon is not how much Bible is used, whether the setting is transferred into our day, or how much language of the Scripture is used, and certainly not whether the passage has determined the structure of the sermon. The test for a biblical sermon is whether the insight of the Word expressed in the passage in that day becomes insight and Word for us in ours. It is not the trappings of the Scripture but the insight or the revelation.

If such is the case, then, the preacher may preach a textual sermon in his or her own way—in any form whatsoever—as long as the intent of the text remains authentic. I once heard a sermon, "On Mature Mindedness," by Dr. Gene E. Bartlett,[7] based on Philippians 3:12–16. In this instance, the text did furnish the basic structure, but in no way was it a static or wooden sermon. The flow of the sermon was derived from three affirmations in the text: (1) "Not that I have obtained this or am already perfect" (vs. 12), (2) "Forgetting what lies behind" (vs. 13), (3) "I press on toward the goal for the prize of the upward call of God in Jesus Christ" (vs. 14). In treating each section in relation to Paul and us, the sermon had psychological impact on the congregation, as well as exegetical and theological authenticity. However, one could preach the same text without the verses forming the structure and still have a viable sermon, perhaps even with the sermon having the same substance. For example, (1) acknowledging limitations (peril of idolatry), (2) recognizing forgiveness (assuaging past guilts), and (3) responding to God's call (growing in faith). Such a variation simply illustrates that one's own creativity, not a prescribed pattern, is what makes a sermon viable and effective.

Perhaps the most puzzling biblical form is the text (usually abstracted from a larger passage) which raises a topic. The difficulty is that without the context the sermon can be either a topic closely related to the Scripture, if serious exegesis is done, or it can simply serve as a springboard for a theme totally unrelated to the Scripture. "Where there is no vision, the people perish" (Prov. 29:18) could be an example of a sermon text totally unrelated to biblical categories. Presumably such a sermon on vision could go all the way from ophthalmology to, "On a Clear Day You Can See Forever." Opening a fortune cookie could provide the same kind of a springboard. Even where there is context, the preacher who abstracts a text and preaches it apart from the setting is often doing an injustice to the passage. A sermon on Philippians 2:5 stated part of the text, "Have this mind in you which was in Christ Jesus," and stopped at that point. The question was then raised as to what kind of a mind Jesus had. Friendly and open were then listed as characteristics of Jesus' mind. Of course, that passage is deeply Christological—the doctrine of *kenosis*—and the heart of the text was ignored: ". . . who, though he was in the form of God, did not count equality with God a thing to be grasped, but emptied himself, taking the form of a servant, being born in the likeness of men."

Or take the account of the Ascension in Acts 1:9. A preacher once preached on, "And a cloud received him out of their sight," and raised the question of what kinds of clouds take Jesus out of our sights. Fear and prejudice were two of the "clouds" that take Jesus out of our "sight" today. There is nothing felonious about such preaching. Figurative preaching has a place, and even clever twists of the text can sometimes be arresting. However, the fault of such preaching is that it may give both the congregation and the preacher the impression that they are hearing and preaching biblical sermons. A sermon that misses the point of the text or simply uses the text as a springboard to an excursion by the minister may occasionally be helpful, but it certainly cannot be labeled biblical.

And yet, such figurative preaching has a hallowed history in the Christian church. Origen is probably our progenitor, when it comes to spawning the offspring of figurative sermons throughout the centuries. To oversimplify, Origen believed the Scriptures to be sacred, so that every literal detail must have some spiritual meaning. He interpreted Scripture and, through the method of allegory, imbued it with spiritual meaning. Though not referring to a specific sermon, an Origen-like sermon would take a scene such as Jesus in a boat with his disciples fishing. The sea would be the world, the fish the sinner, the net the gospel, the tiller the church, etc. Luther was critical of such allegorical use of the Scriptures.

> We see that Jerome, Origen and other ancient writers did not employ a sufficiently felicitous and helpful method of devising allegories, since they direct everything to manners and works, whereas everything should rather be applied to the Word and to faith.
> . . . it is a proper allegory when, so far as possible, they discover in every allegory the ministry of the Word or the progress of the Gospel and of faith.[8]

For Luther, it was not the *words* of the Scripture but the *Word* coming through the *words* that engendered faith.

The Bible is filled with parables, stories, and incidents, many of which do introduce figures of speech and analogies. The Gospel of John is filled with such figures: with the woman at the well Jesus spoke of living water; at the wedding feast at Cana he made water into wine; the healing stories use interesting figures of blindness and sight. John 10 introduces the figure of sheep—a figure that seems mixed: first, the sheepfold; second, the shepherd enters the door, but there is also a gatekeeper; then Jesus says he is the door of the sheep; then Jesus is the shepherd; and finally, Jesus as the shepherd lays down his life for the sheep. This latter figure reminds us of Isaiah 53:6–7:

> All we like sheep have gone astray;
>   we have turned every one to his own way;
> and the LORD has laid on him
>   the iniquity of us all.
> He was oppressed, and he was afflicted,
>   yet he opened not his mouth;
> like a lamb that is led to the slaughter,
>   and like a sheep that before its shearers is dumb,
> so he opened not his mouth.

When figures such as this one become mixed, is it any wonder that congregations can get confused? Worse still, preachers preach on such passages without trying to unscramble the meaning of an analogy; unfortunately, perhaps, not even seeing the problem. For the preacher, the most important verse in John 10 may be, "this figure Jesus used with them, but they did not understand what he was saying to them" (vs. 6). That is obviously as true for the modern disciples as for the ancient ones. Though John is filled with such figures of speech, the entire Bible has similar metaphors, allegories, and parables which need illuminating by the preacher.

Again, the specific form or shape of the sermon is not nearly as important as the fact that the sermon has movement and progression, which a form provides. There are many books in preaching which will give patterns of development for sermons. The advanced preacher often scoffs at outlines, but the beginning student seeking help finds suggested patterns a way of getting started, before developing his or her own method. By themselves, "types" of sermons can seem sterile, but a novitiate may need some guidance in the beginning. Surprisingly, what looks like a sterile outline may come alive in the hands of a dedicated preacher. Some preachers respond naturally to preaching texts and themes along the lines of dialectic or paradoxical patterns. Many of our gospel affirmations lend themselves to such treatment. When we affirm Jesus as human *and* divine, for example, we can see how Christological sermons might employ such a method.

In short, there are undoubtedly creative preachers who resist form and structure, though an amazing number of those have to write and become dependent upon manuscripts. At the same time, the student of preaching should learn the discipline of struggling with an idea and seeking a form to express it. Indeed, the form of a creative idea is in the idea. Occasionally, one will find a preacher who says that he or she has creative ideas but has trouble organizing them in a form. A wise colleague once reacted to that by stating that "they really do not have the idea." Each idea—however creative—has within it and, indeed, indistinguishable from the idea, the form. Whatever the type of sermon, whatever the creative thinking that has engendered the idea, it either evolves into some form or else the idea itself is unclear—not only to the congregation—but often to the preacher. To paraphrase Paul, "If I speak in the tongues of men and of angels, but have not *clarity*, I am a sounding brass and tinkling cymbal" (I Cor. 13:1 KJV). A clear thesis and a shape that allows people to move with the sermon go a long way towards insuring that the gospel is neither meaningless nor without form and void.

7

Forms That Allow Movement

Though Phillips Brooks long ago defined preaching as "bringing truth through personality,"[1] that concept, rightly considered, can cause anxiety for many theological students and parish ministers. On the one hand, we can admit that in some way we are dealing with the Word of God in preaching (though even that idea is frightening when we see the Word as that which is incarnated in our words). On the other hand, the thought that we ourselves embody that Word in some significant way in our person can be threatening—especially to those who are new to ministry or to those who have never thought through the import of such a claim. This anxiety might be called the ontology of preaching—my being vis-à-vis the pulpit. Such a thought engenders *angst* in those who are aware of the seriousness of the claims made by speaking the Word of God and doing it through oneself as integral to the Word itself.

Though one might cringe at the thought that "*you* are the sermon," the concept is not limited to religious discourse. In modern form it can be McLuhan's "the medium is the message,"[2] and it is as ancient as Aristotle's *Rhetoric*. Aristotle contended that the greatest factor in persuasion was the *ethos* of the speaker. That is, what emanated from the speaker—even limited to the speech occasion—was the most important factor in believability. For him, ethical persuasion was made up of three components: *intelligence, character,* and *good will*. Another way to state these would be *competence, virtue,* and *good will*. Whatever the labels, these categories are easily transferable into parallels for preaching, as homileticians have done all through history, from St. Augustine to the present. Restating the concepts in another framework can show the relevance for proclamation. It is clear that the personality, pastoral skills, and the general attitude of the preacher are being communicated in the sermon, both vocally and nonvocally. This means that what she or he is as a pastor, spouse, parent, and administrator is being communicated both on the audible and inaudible levels during a worship service.

Since *intelligence* is too often read as academic prowess reserved for highly educated clergy, *competence* may have better connotations for ministers. *Competence* seems self-explanatory, but we do not always consider that as a factor of our person which is being communicated both in the sermon verbally and also below the threshold of audibility. In blunt terms, it means that a preacher who has not worked sufficiently on the sermon, is unclear in ideas, chooses subjects that are irrelevant to the people's needs, is unkempt in grammar, and makes grossly generalized statements would be reflecting as poor an ethos as a preacher who was immoral. No amount of piety or even sincerity will counteract the lack of competence on the part of the preacher.

Phillips Brooks tells a fascinating story of his first few days in a Virginia seminary. He had come from a background where students at college studied hard but said little about faith. In seminary he became acquainted with a prayer meeting for the first time and was greatly impressed by the devoutness of the students. He felt inadequate. The next day in Greek class, however, many of the same pious students were unprepared for their lessons. He suggests they had not learned "hard, faithful, conscientious study." He concludes by suggesting that, "the boiler [passion] had no connection with the engine [intellect]."[3]

Though both the *boiler* and the *engine* are necessary in preaching and affect ethos, there is no doubt that faith—however pious—will not remove the necessity for professional competency in ministry.

Character in Aristotle's sense can be misleading. In some ways, all of ethos is character. *Virtue* might be a better term, even for Aristotle. To change character to *authenticity* or *integrity* would be even more accurate for our purposes. Character is too often interpreted by religionists in simplistic or moralistic terms. In a pluralistic church Christians may differ in theology, lifestyles, and ways of expressing faith. The key point of ethos is, does this person "ring true"? Does he or she sound like an honest person speaking? The old saying that "what you are speaks so loud that I cannot hear what you are saying" is one way to address that aspect of ethos. A comic calendar had one day of the week labeled, "Blyme's Formula for Success: The secret of Success is sincerity. Once you can fake that, you've got it made." The truth is, of course, that one cannot fake sincerity—at least for long.

Basically, ethos can be stated succinctly. What we are as persons, friends, spouses, parents, administrators, and pastors is being communicated on Sunday morning—if not vocally, certainly nonvocally. The sermon never begins at eleven o'clock on Sunday. The totality of the person preaching is part of the preaching event itself. Sometimes that may seem unfair, for we all have our worst moments; nevertheless, we are communicating what we are. If we are hostile, defensive, or angry, that will be coming through regardless of the content of the sermon. If we have stained-glass voices in the pulpit or are sentimentally pious or condescending, that, too, will be coming through. It is not that we must relinquish our own integrity and authenticity, nor does it mean we must give up being fully human. Simply put, it means our lives are of one piece. In parish terms, it means that one is a good pastor before being a good preacher. At least they go hand-in-hand. What we are on Saturday, the congregation sees on Sunday. We do not need to become sycophants. We can preach with authority without being authoritarian. Nor do we expect ministers to be perfect, without flaw, without faults. However, the preacher who has a healthy attitude toward self and others—providing he or she has a message—is really the persuasive preacher.

Good will according to Aristotle concerned disposition and emotions. For us, it can be seen as the disposition of the preacher toward the congregation and the concern for them manifested both in being the preacher, the attitude radiated toward them, and the language spoken to the people. Further, it is the empathy established by how well the preacher reads the dispositions and emotions of the congregation. In short, do they read the preacher as having rapport with them by what they perceive, and does the preacher read accurately the feelings and situation of the congregation? This is the attitude that makes the preaching moment dialogical. It is the care and concern that manifests itself in knowledge of the people and where their needs are. Of course, it does not mean catering to their whims or withholding what Kyle Haselden called both the "Peril and Promise of the gospel."[4] Louis XIV was reported to have said to Massilon, the great court preacher, "Father, I have heard in this chapel many great orators, and have been much pleased with them; but whenever I have heard you, I have been displeased with myself."[5] Even the prophetic word, then, can reveal an empathy for the congregation. Indeed, that empathy is a precondition for a prophetic word.

Competence (or intelligence), authenticity (or integrity), and good will may seem simply secular categories if related only to classical rhetoric. However, when we come back to where we began—that we deal with the Word of God in preaching—then such concepts take on meaning. If the thought of the pulpit and its importance strike awe in our hearts, we can be comforted by the incarnational aspect of preaching in the same way we take comfort in the incarnation itself. Kendrick Grobel once said, speaking of Bultmann's commitment to preaching, "to a true Lutheran there are no 'great preachers' (are there any to a true *Christian?*) but only responsible and less responsible ones."[6] If we are faithful, we can come to terms with the fact that we are instruments, not the progenitors, of the gospel. We need not feel as destitute as Rev. Mr. Dimmesdale in *The Scarlet Letter*, who "only wondered that Heaven should see fit to transmit the grand and solemn music of its oracles through so foul an organ-pipe as he."[7] We can feel, however, that what we are and who we are are inextricably tied to both the nature of the gospel and its proclamation. "Preaching," as Fred Craddock reminds us, can be properly defined as both "that which is preached" and "the act of presenting the Gospel."[8] However, there is a great deal of difference between being a "little Jesus" and Luther's "Christ to the neighbor." We are not models in the sense of the former, but we are mandated as Christ's people in the latter.

C. H. Dodd long ago made the strong case that the paradigm for the preacher was a town crier, an auctioneer, a herald (*keryx*), the one who brought the good news (*kerygma*), but it was a message from the King, not the messenger. According to Dodd, "*kerygma* signifies not the action of the preacher, but that which he preaches, his 'message.' "[9] Ebeling,[10] perhaps reflecting the Germans' love of the American West, uses the word, *deputy*. And, Paul, of course, uses the word *ambassador*. To be sure, in the latter instances, the messenger is not the author of the message, but bringing the message and telling the message are part and parcel of the message.

> He has reconciled us men to himself through Christ, and he has enlisted us in this service of reconciliation. What I mean is, that God was in Christ reconciling the world to himself, no longer holding men's misdeeds against them, and that he has entrusted us with the message of reconciliation. We come therefore as Christ's ambassadors. It is as if God were appealing to you through us: in Christ's name, we implore you, be reconciled to God!
> (2 Cor 5:18–20 NEB)

To be reconcilers, to be entrusted with the message of reconciliation, to implore others to be reconciled to God, and to sense that God is using us to appeal to others, all state succinctly what the proclaimer does. Though such a mandate should not seem more frightening than what is required of any Christian witness, there is still awe of the pulpit and the theological import of carrying God's Word, which make preachers uncomfortable at times. The theological weight of a witness does not seem as heavy as the burden the preacher senses, when the Word of God and speaking in God's name to a congregation are combined.

As suggested, part of this burden is theological, and some, of course, is the overwhelming consciousness of our role in the gospel as preachers. To know that the sermon is revealing us can be threatening psychologically, as well as theologically. We cannot hide who we are—at least for long. Manuscripts, robes, pulpits, language, delivery can be used as masks to hide who we are, but they are simply "masks," and the true self will be made known—sooner or later—and if that self is different from the projected self, then the ethos of the preacher is undermined. The real self will be communicated nonvocally or subliminally, if not overtly, and the congregation will discover the discrepancy between that self and the projected, "professionally-ministerial" self, even though they may not be able to articulate it clearly.

There is, of course, another side to the "masking" of the self. There are ministers, who, in the diminution of the Word of God, go to the other extreme and seem to make themselves the focus of the sermon. Rather than sensing the awe of the pulpit, it becomes a place for personal testimony and witness, even though labeled "sermon." They see themselves as too much embodying the gospel and too little emphasizing *the* Word. Sermons become "I" centered, dramatizing of self, and preaching is thought to be a telling of stories—often of the preacher's experience. This should not be compared with the interest in narrative, parable, and story which is being emphasized today, even though there may be similarities. A recent book, which has excellent material otherwise, gives credence to some of this personal preaching. "You must risk telling your own story, not as an end in itself, but rather as a sharply focused lens through which the whole Christian story is refracted."[11] The key is "not as an end in itself." My story or my preacher's story is only of worth if it illustrates or embodies *the Story*. Also, does my minister—or any minister—have the ability or experience to have stories that can "refract" the entire gospel? Testimony and witness are not proclamation and preaching.

Preachers sometimes have problems with their role in the preaching process, for fear of being advocates. We are nervous about being authoritarian, dogmatic, and espousing too strong a position as an advocate. We understand the reluctance when we see the abuses. We also see the change in education and communication regarding group dynamics, problem-solving, and group process. Ernest Campbell vividly describes this attitude:

> Some almost apologize for having to do it [preaching]. Deeply branded by Group Dynamics and convinced of the virtues of the round table, they preach from back on their heels, rather than up on their toes. "Nobody listening, I hope, I hope, I hope." These pitiable professionals have been utterly faked out of any confidence that preaching matters.[12]

Evidently for us it is difficult to see how one can preach Christian dogma without being dogmatic, to be an advocate without being argumentative, to preach with authority without being authoritarian. Here again, it is the attitude of the proclaimer which is basic to the process. As post-baptized, post-resurrection Christians, we are advocates. The world in which we live is not made of people with no opinions but of persons with contending opinions. Those of us who are Christians and believers are advocates. Our being and Christian symbols reveal that advocacy. Our words are tools we use in advocating. Preachers are expected to use words authoritatively. However, they are not expected to be authoritarian—that quality displays the inadequacy of the proclaimer.

Psychologically, all of us are nervous about revealing our internality—particularly that which might seem to us a fault. The fear of revealing ourselves radiates from our theological uncertainties and our personal weaknesses. We may be hesitant to discuss our theological doubts, the areas of Christian faith that lack certitude, and the questions we ourselves have about certain Christian affirmations. How can we dare reveal too much of what we really think and feel and still remain in the parish and pulpit? Incredibly, though, there is another side to these fears. A belief, for example, is really a belief—has been appropriated viscerally—when we have been able to articulate it. This says that what we do believe and what we can affirm can give us both confidence and satisfaction when we do speak. Then we hear ourselves say what we believe. It becomes ours, and we can feel positive about it. Further, dialogue with the text or even some aspect of faith is a stance that congregations appreciate. Preachers who are honest with the text that troubles them often find ready responses from those who, too, have wrestled with Scripture and faith. The very honesty of the preacher manifests his or her integrity; hence, the strengthening of one's ethos. Coming to terms with one's own authenticity in belief and person can actually be therapeutic, for to be accepted finally for who one really is can be wholesome for one's faith and being.

Years ago, depending upon the church denomination and the theology, the preacher's presence was minimized, the preacher becoming a mere channel or conduit through which the message from God flowed. Though the intent was important, the results could make preaching highly sacramental with the minister's place minimized. Dr. John Watson (Ian Maclaren), a famous preacher of another day, once commented, "As it now appears to me, the chief effect of every sermon should be to unveil Christ, and the chief art of the preacher to conceal himself."[13] Though this "high" view of preaching could use emphasis, no doubt, in any day, a more realistic view of the preacher's role comes from the scholar Eduard Schweizer, who wrote, "It is all the more apparent that the messenger's personal authority and integrity must be believed in if his preaching is actually to bring salvation and judgment and not just remain a theological lecture."[14]

Our being, then, is integral to the content of the gospel and the preaching of the gospel. Martin Buber tells the story of one who came before the master, the Maggid, and saw him on his bed. It was the master's *will* that he observed; in him he saw the *will* of the Most High. Buber concludes that, "That was why his disciples learned even more and greater things from his sheer *being* than from his *words*" (italics mine).[15] This does not mean that words do not matter, but it does illustrate the importance of one's *being*. Or as one author, who talks about the difficulty of the Christian vocabulary for communication in our day, observes, "people have learned to pay . . . careful attention . . . to *who* it is that says something."[16] One could amend that somewhat more accurately by saying that in addition to hearing what is being said, congregations look for who is talking as well.

The preacher, then, without being irreverent, can say as of an earlier incarnation, "The Word became flesh and dwelt among us." So, the Word becomes flesh in the person and words of the preacher. This is in no way an arrogant stance. Will Willimon makes the incarnation point vivid in our day: "The Word is never simply interesting information, noble ideas, or historical data. The Word is personal, a Person confronting persons, incarnational, in the flesh."[17]

8

How Shall They Hear
Without a Preacher?

One needs to be hesitant about being dogmatic in regard to delivery. Some preachers are direct, avoiding the use of manuscripts or notes altogether. Others speak from notes, while still others use manuscripts. Some write out their sermons, whether the manuscripts are used in the pulpit or not. Some write and then read the sermons. Some never write anything. Preachers using each category above and other styles not mentioned are very effective preachers. At the same time, there are both communicative and rhetorical principles which undergird the effective presentation of any style or type of sermon.

Since this book is on homiletics, and not specifically speech communication, there is no need to list in detail all the elements of effective delivery. Other books are available to fill that need.[1] For our purposes, there are several significant areas that can be emphasized for the presentation of any sermon. These concerns undergird all styles of proclamation, and since preaching is a unique creation, the model developed by the preacher will and should be individual.

There is no doubt that one of the primary places a sermon often fails is in its delivery. An otherwise good sermon dies on the runway when the preacher does not have the thrust to get it off the ground. There could be many reasons for this, all the way from poor voice quality, to faulty enunciation, lack of fluency, and meager enthusiasm. Whatever the specific reasons, the major fault is that with most sermons not enough time is spent between the finishing of the sermon and its presentation. Whether it is the disciplined preacher who affirms he or she is finished with the sermon by Friday noon, the preacher who spends all day Saturday putting it together, or the preacher who is harried all week and can get it together just about any time right up until Sunday morning, the problem is still the same. Many preachers do not consciously spend time planning how this sermon will be delivered orally. Whether manuscript, outlines, notes, or some other form, the admonition here is to spend time consciously on delivering the sermon. This could go all the way from preaching it aloud in the pulpit to dictating it into a tape recorder and listening to the tape, speaking it aloud in one's study, or simply going over it silently but thinking orally. Many of us feel so relieved when the sermon is finished that we do not worry too much about its delivery. We depend upon the moment to "bring it alive" before the congregations' eyes. The sermon becomes a lifeless "thing" to which we give mouth-to-mouth resuscitation in front of the congregation. Many preachers, of course, seem to do well with this process, but most of us will be more effective if we have prepared specifically for the presentation.

The basic question to ask is this: is the "thing" that we have toiled over all week, prepared carefully, outlined, written out, and pulled out of the typewriter with relief really *the* sermon? Surely not. A composer works assiduously over a piece of music, perhaps writing words, finding melodies, putting in chords, deciding on the number of parts, perhaps going into counterpoint, writing a fuller accompaniment, and deciding upon instrumentation, arriving finally at pages of score upon his or her desk or piano. However, in no way could that piece of music now seen on score paper, after several weeks of work, be considered the anthem, song, or cantata. It is such only when it has been sung by a choir or chorus, no matter how many are in it or how good or bad the presentation. The anthem is the "coming alive" in the singing and the hearing. Before that, the music is in the composer's head and in the notes on paper.[2] The similarity to the sermon is striking. The sermon written or put together in the study is not the sermon. The minister may have a manuscript, notes on a sermon, the ideas of the sermon, an outline for a sermon, but the sermon is the event when it is delivered in the worship setting in the midst of a congregation. It is for that reason that the preparation for the presentation may be the most important key in the entire process of evolving a sermon. Again, it is not the length of time spent but the *necessity* of time spent—the *qualitative* over the *quantitative* time.

Naturally following the concern for the presentation of the sermon and integral to it is the recognition that the sermon on Sunday morning is really an event which belongs to a larger event—the totality of the worship service. This is another reason why care with the presentation of the sermon is so significant. Specifically, this says several things to the preacher. The attitude of the minister in the entire worship service, including how it is led and how the preacher participates in it, would be a factor. The content and its relevance to the congregation are important. One should ask if the material is only on the cognitive level, or is it presented existentially or holistically—reaching the congregation on multilevels of their being—mind, heart, will, volitional levels? As is true for ethos, are the attitude, voice, bodily action involved in the sermon's communication? Body language has more and more come into our consciousness in recent years. Our body language often strengthens and accompanies our words in delivering God's Word. On the other hand, our body language may be contradicting our ideas and thoughts. In other cases, our bodies do not seem to be involved at all.

Many preachers in the so-called "mainline" churches tend to treat the material and their people only on the cognitive level. Part of that, of course, is the nervousness they have in showing their own deep feelings, and often it is because they have been rightly skeptical of emotionalism exhibited in churches of their youth, on television, or in a variety of churches in the present scene. The revulsion towards emotion in place of thought has led them to confuse emotion with emotionalism, sentiment with sentimentality, and the result has been a retreat entirely from the affective level in themselves and in their preaching, finally resting their preaching, if not their lives, on the cognitive level alone. Saul Bellow, the novelist, comments upon a certain group of literary intellectuals: "for feeling or response they substitute acts of comprehension."³ Pulpits galore substitute acts of comprehension for feelings or affective responses. The bottom line is that unless we are reaching people on all levels—mind, heart, will—we are not even communicating, let alone motivating.

To be sure, the affective level is a tricky area of communication, but avoiding it is not the answer. Undoubtedly, there are preachers who devote their lives and preaching to wallowing in people's emotions, attempting to stir them to responses, occasionally deliberately manipulating them for effect, and conceiving of the gospel themselves as deep feelings of a highly personal nature. Much of such religion surely depends upon one's psychological make-up as much as it does on one's theological beliefs. The problem with this approach is that the appeal to human minds is often avoided. Whatever else the gospel is, it should make sense to the believer. And, the preacher who wishes to preach in our day needs to appeal to people's minds as well as their hearts. Remember Phillips Brooks' words, already used in another connection, that the boiler must be connected to the engine. A boiler-room depth of feeling and heat will not be enough, unless the engines of human minds are turned over by the power engendered. A major part of the totality of the preaching-event is the joining of the affective and cognitive.

The very fact of preaching is much more than carrying the content of the gospel. The *bringing* of the gospel (or the *telling* of the story) is indispensable to the gospel or story itself. Indeed, it is part of the gospel itself. It is important, then, for the preacher to begin to think orally from the very beginning of the sermon process. Clyde Fant used the word "orascript" in contradistinction to the "manuscript."⁴ It is a distinction worth making. Most of us have a writing style that differs from a spoken style. We write literarily, and we speak conversationally. Except in rare instances, the two are not synonymous. Thus, even if a minister is relatively free in delivery, he or she has often spent most of the week working on notes, outline, and manuscript—all of which may be in a style different from what is delivered. Both in terms of what preaching is and what a sermon is, for many it would take a revolutionary step to begin from the first moment of preparation to think orally. One effective minister I know does not write anything on paper any longer, and even the exegesis is thought through orally or talked through. The entire development is oral from the beginning. Others would do a great amount of writing, taking notes, making outlines, and even writing manuscripts, but the key emphasis would be that each step was an oral one. When it comes to delivery, the task is not to take a manuscript and make it oral but to deliver to the congregation that which has been oral all the time, from inception to that moment when the sermon begins in the pulpit. Though no one should diminish the importance of style and writing effectively, both of which have their own persuasive powers, it does seem clear that in the final analysis the gospel itself (the message) and the bringing of the gospel (the messenger) and the congregation (receivers) should receive the primary attention and emphasis.

Communicatively, then, delivery is important precisely because of the nature of the gospel: it is a preached or proclaimed Word. The *bringing* is as important as the *bringer*. The *telling* is as important as the *teller*. The temptation to keep the mind/body dualism is always present. Some preachers who say nothing well are sometimes considered to be good communicators. Others emphasize the content, minimizing delivery factors as mere rhetoric or techniques. In truth, for the same reason that communication effectively pursued is holistic, so is the preaching act. The preacher who emphasizes delivery to the exclusion of the message is a showperson who forgot the importance of the gospel. The preacher who ridicules delivery because the content is primary usually affirms that when you have something to say, how to say it is unimportant. The former is a Sophist; the latter misunderstands the gospel, assuming it is a body of content, and does not realize that the bringing of the gospel is part and parcel of the gospel itself.

While this book does not purport to be a book of techniques for effective preaching nor a book covering all aspects of homiletics, it is important to point out the significant and important areas for emphasis. There are other books[5] which go into detail on such matters as affective communication of a sermon or speech. Our concern is with basic principles more than with an effort to redo communication for preachers. At the same time, and close to the body/mind dualism seen above, a host of ministers seem to have trouble accepting the role of their bodies and dedicating them to God's work. To talk about a "call" to preach—a devotion to God and the church—seems quite clear to most preachers. However, to assume that the entire person is dedicated and used in ministry seems foreign. Yet, it is this very commitment of the whole person that is the basic reason for concern with the delivery of a sermon and attention to those gifts, talents, and skills with which we are endowed.

We have already seen how the preaching event is holistic. It follows naturally that all parts of body/content/spirit/commitment are mutually involved in preaching. The voice, to take one example, can be detrimental to the event as well as positive. One's voice, if operating properly, will enhance the effectiveness of the sermon, not because of its mellifluousness or resonance but largely because it does not stand out—it is a non-factor. Contrariwise, a voice operating improperly will stand out and distract. Many of us breathe improperly when we speak. That not only causes breathiness but usually throatiness and lack of resonance. "Belly" breathing is not the answer to the world's problems, but a human being who has been given gifts by God should endeavor to use those gifts properly, especially if preaching the gospel. An incarnational view of communication does not mean glorying in our liabilities without dedicated usage. Voices that are monotonous or ministerial can be distracting. Poor enunciation and grammar interfere with the bringing of the message. One's ethos is often harmed by such inadequacies. None of this means that all preachers should sound alike. We do not need to have preachers come into the ministry as though created from cookie cutters. Each minister is his or her own person with a unique style in delivery as in everything else. The call is for honing one's skills, whatever talents we have been given.

The role of body language has been seen in connection with the totality of the preaching experience. If the total participation of the preacher in the sermon is demanded, then obviously the physical attributes are present. This is undoubtedly one reason why many ministers leave manuscripts behind, move out of the pulpit, and come closer to their congregations. Though those specific instances have problems in themselves for other reasons, there is the imperative for some to participate fully in the preaching moment, other than with just head and voice. The key to remember about the body was hinted at under ethos.

The body language may be saying something completely different than the words being uttered. Part of that body language is, of course, gestures. Without enumerating the variety of gestures and their meaning, it is enough to say that if gestures are properly motivated from what is being said—both content and mood—and are not distracting, then the form, amount, or kind of gesturing would be irrelevant. Our facial expressions, and especially our eye contact, are essentially of the same order.

The bottom line is how communicative we are. Since communion and communication are not too far apart in their root meaning, and certainly not in their intent, it is not too much to suggest that an incarnational view of communication is the preacher extending himself or herself to the congregation in an effort to be genuinely present in every respect. The key question may be: how communicative or eager to share is the preacher in relation to the people? This question takes precedence over what the preacher is wearing, what kind of manuscript or notes are in the pulpit, or where the preacher stands. Does the sermon have the ring of honest talk? Does it sound like a real person talking to real people? In short, why should we not expect rigor in delivery, as we do in exegesis?

Another area that concerns delivery vitally is the beginning and ending of the sermon. Whether we are talking about Aristotle's aesthetics in regard to beginning, middle, and end or whether someone might feel that there is a Hegelian pattern built into most of life, there seems little doubt that public speeches of all kinds have a beginning, a middle, and an end. This is in contrast to the three points, a poem, and a prayer that many aver are taught in seminaries and are the paradigm sermon for most preachers. Movement or progression simply starts and ends no matter what else may be going on. Since we are told constantly that people listen in the beginning, though only long enough to see if their attention is to be captured by something worthwhile, then the introduction may need specific attention by the preacher who seeks to invite his or her congregation into the gospel. The same can be said for the ending. People listen or listen again when the preacher gets to the conclusion. Any preacher can note this phenomenon when "finally" is proclaimed from the pulpit. Faces light up, the attention is aroused, and expectations are there for the finish. However, the preacher can also note the disappointment in the faces of the congregation when they feel betrayed as the sermon does not end but trudges on and on after what they have perceived psychologically as the end of the sermon.

Granted that an introduction and a conclusion are content-wise indispensable and unified elements of a sermon, they nevertheless have separate functions which merit our attention under delivery. Even though the old saw that people listen for the first few seconds of an oral presentation may be overdrawn, there is little doubt that in the beginning they are attuned to hear. That openness can be dissipated quickly if their attention is not held and maintained. The ideas of the sermon to be addressed, unfortunately, are not enough. We should take people where they are, not where we would like for them to be. In oral communion with the listeners, we enter into their lives in order to be genuinely present to them. We not only have a message to proclaim, but we capture the interest that is dominant in the beginning and try to involve the people in the importance of the theme. This certainly does not mean manipulating them, pandering them by trying to be entertaining in order to win approval, or seeking to arrest attention at the expense of the subject matter. It does mean taking our congregation seriously and relating the material to the hearers.

Underlying the significance of an introduction are two principles of communication and homiletics which, if operative in a given sermon, can enhance the beginning. The form an introduction may take can vary, but if an introduction first arouses interest or arrests attention, and then discloses and clarifies the subject, the introduction has a basis for being effective. There is no particular model for the shape of an introduction as to its form and content. Each preacher will and should develop his or her own. According to the first principle, the sermon should arrest attention, and there are many ways to do that. Though many books deal with a variety of introductions, for our purposes we can tabulate only a few of the different ways.

A sermon with a striking statement can go a long way toward capturing the interest of a congregation. "Half of the world's population is going to bed hungry tonight," or "For our age there are but two alternatives. Either the point of a gun or the foot of the Cross," are examples of striking statements that can arrest attention, assuming, of course, that they lead into the sermon itself. A stirring quotation will also command attention. Questions can be effective if two things are remembered. First, too many raised in an introduction can be discursive, and second, the speaker who raises a good many questions in an introduction has an obligation to deal with them. Questions, for questions' sake, can divert listeners from the main theme of the sermon when too many are introduced. Still, even a simple question like, "Have you ever thought about what it really means to be a Christian?" can arrest attention and focus the theme. A Harry Emerson Fosdick could very well begin a sermon with something arresting like, "Can a modern person believe in God?" Assuming, again, that the questions not only arouse interest but lead to a theme that deals with that question, then this form of introduction has merit.

In our day, with the special interest in narrative, parable, and story, narration is a good way to begin. To tell a biblical story in one's own words or to tell a modern story that lends itself to Christian insight can be most effective. To retell some of the well-known or not so familiar biblical or Christian stories can embrace a congregation effectively and immediately. John Steinbeck, in *East of Eden*, doing the Cain and Abel story, should encourage the modern preacher to put in his or her own words the same story. Or, taking a modern story that may lead to the good news can lead a congregation psychologically into the denouement of a Christian proclamation. Isaac Bashevis Singer or John Cheever has the ability to raise human drama to the narrative form, which models not only the form and style, but which speaks to our condition in this age. Close to the use of narrative is the employment of dialogue in preaching. To take an incident in the Bible, for example, such as Paul in front of Agrippa, and set up the trial scene—not in a theatrical way, but through suggestion and imagination—can involve a congregation in the sermon almost immediately by inviting them "into the picture."

One facet of introductory material remains, and it is the one most often used. Indeed, one might expect to begin there—with a text or biblical material. At the outset it should be noted that a sermon may not get to biblical materials for twenty seconds or twenty minutes and still be an expository or biblical sermon. The amount of biblical language, the placement of biblical material, or beginning with a text has little to do with whether the sermon is biblical or not. At the same time, even if biblical material is used in the beginning and throughout the sermon, the same principle will hold for commanding attention. Assuming that the congregation is ready and willing to begin where the preacher is or ready to jump into Jeremiah is wrong both communicatively and psychologically. Fosdick put it succinctly when he wrote, "Only the preacher proceeds still upon the idea that folk come to church desperately anxious to discover what happened to Jebusites."[6] A text or biblical incident that has arresting qualities can be effective as an introduction. If it does not have them, then it can fail to capture interest. "Those who do not take up the cross and follow me," can be very arresting as part of an opening sentence as well as a text if it is held out in front for all to see, hear, and contemplate. The point is that the biblical material *per se* will not bring the congregation to attention. It will still need to be arrestingly cast and presented.

The second principle can be stated easily, and perhaps is obvious, but it is not only important, it is imperative. No matter how arresting, exciting, humorous, and arousing the introduction, if it does not lead into the sermon's intent, then it has failed. An introduction disjointed from the sermon, as an entity by itself only to arouse interest, has failed. Indeed, it can often be insulting to the intelligence of the congregation if stories are told, jokes mouthed, or personal anecdotes are given merely to "warm up" the congregation before the serious work begins. Though, as we have seen, arresting attention is vital to a good introduction, the more important of the two principles is the revealing and clarifying of the matter of the sermon. However, the two really belong together, and the preacher who weekly captures the attention of the congregation and gets into the material as if it were all of one piece, has created a favorable climate of receptivity, whatever the form or content of the sermon.

Two other matters about introductions should be noted in connection with delivery. First, many sermons take too long to get started. Preachers have a proclivity for spending too much time in the beginning. There are undoubtedly manifold reasons for such long introductions. As we have seen, some want to "warm up" the congregation under the guise of establishing rapport. Still others feel they are laying groundwork for what comes later. Since it is easier to set up problems, diagnose issues, and raise questions than it is to solve problems, prescribe courses of action, and deal responsibly with the issues and questions, we preachers have the tendency to have large amounts of introductory material (setting up issues and analyzing problems) and very little of soteriology (prescription and gospel affirmation). Sin is easier to describe than grace, or at least we have more examples of the former. Preachers would be served well if they took time to review sermons they have preached in order to see the length of time it has taken them to get into the sermon. One preacher has suggested that our preaching would be more effective if the last part of the sermon took fifty per cent of the sermon itself. Of course, the preacher may consciously want to "preach *to* the subject or thesis," as in a controversial sermon, but the admonition still holds. The introduction that is arresting and leads to the subject can often gain impact if the congregation gets into it without too much delay.

The other concern for the introduction's effectiveness, though fraught with some danger, can be most positive. Assuming that the congregation tends to listen in the beginning to a speaker's remarks, hoping to have its attention arrested, it follows that ministers should keep the introduction in mind. This indicates that he or she should know exactly what is going to be said. For some this might mean memorization, for others the discipline of committing both content and rhetoric to repetitious thought in the study, and still for others it might mean verbalization in the pulpit. The crucial point is to take seriously, communicatively, and psychologically the beginning of the sermon. Preachers who circuitously wander into their sermons have difficulty taking their people with them. Focused attention in the introduction may set up the climate, at least, for a congregation to follow the sermon with interest and, indeed, be involved in it.

If the introduction is one major point of the sermon where content and delivery are close in importance, the same could be said for the conclusion. The conclusion of the sermon can do many things in theory: end the sermon, motivate the people, call them to action, summarize the ideas, make an application, or challenge the congregation to commitment. As in the introduction, there are a variety of forms and styles of conclusion.[7] Perhaps the central, and most important, function of the conclusion is to end the sermon. That seems so obvious, but preachers notoriously have a difficult time stopping. How many congregations suffer week after week with a preacher who misses several opportunities to quit? Some even give false endings, stating, "In conclusion," or "Finally," or "In sum," several times before finally dragging the sermon to its ending. To paraphrase T.S. Eliot, the sermon ends not with a bang but with a whimper.

Though a conclusion can surely have a variety of purposes and functions, and myriad styles and forms, it is in keeping with the thrust of this book to suggest that a most effective conclusion—whatever the form and style—is one that dramatizes the thesis. Again, assuming that an effective sermon is one that has an underlying thesis—a one-sentence affirmation of what the sermon is proclaiming, then a conclusion that dramatizes the thesis may be the most important thing that can be done. Such a principle leaves room for creative ways of formulating a conclusion. Suppose, for example, a preacher had as a thesis for a sermon, "When we give ourselves in faith to God, we become new persons." How could he or she dramatize such an idea? There are many ways other than stating it didactically. Apart from the exclusive language, one way which illustrates the point being made is the following parable which C.S. Lewis borrowed from George MacDonald:

> Imagine ourselves as a living house. God comes in to rebuild that house. At first, perhaps, you can understand what He's doing. He's getting the drains right and stopping the leaks in the roof and so on: you knew that those jobs needed doing and so you are not surprised. But presently he starts knocking the house about in a way that hurts abominably and does not seem to make sense. What on earth is He up to? The explanation is that He is building quite a different house from the one you thought of—throwing out a new wing here, putting on an extra floor there, running up towers, making courtyards. You thought you were going to be made into a decent little cottage: but He is building a *palace*. He intends to come and live in it Himself.[8]

If the preacher can resist the temptation to explain what it means, then the implications of this type of conclusion can be left to the congregation who has seen the picture and perhaps even entered into it existentially. The grievous fault, of course, is the temptation to add on, to explain what it all means. The point is pounded into the ground, and the congregation has had its moment of imagination and self-discovery dissipated.

The strength of dramatizing the thesis as a conclusion is that it not only ends the sermon but in its own way summarizes, motivates, and makes the application as the main point of the sermon is lifted up and vivified. Such a conclusion is limitless in the shape it may take. An illustration, a hypothetical incident, a vignette out of church history, a true story, a quotation, or even a hymn may be employed to make the ending have an impact on the sermon in the minds and hearts of the congregation. It is this latter which is significantly important. The conclusion which dramatizes the idea has the fortunate role of being able to join together the cognitive and affective in an imaginative way.

Delivery, then, has a broad scope. By itself it can be seen as simply communicative skills or techniques. In terms of proclamation, it can be seen as integral to the gospel itself and decisive for the response of commitment on the part of listeners.

9

The Sermon Event: Preaching

Kierkegaard's oft-used analogy furnishes one way of seeing the context of worship and the relationship between the Word delivered and the congregation, not only as receivers but as participants. Kierkegaard's point was that Christians go to church as they go to the theater. They sit back and listen to the preaching, making judgments as to the sermon's effectiveness and evaluating the preacher's ability. In truth, says Kierkegaard, the worship service for the Christian should be quite the opposite. It is the congregation which is on the "stage," the preacher is the "prompter," and the "audience" is God, the Critic-Judge. Such a figure is one way to consider the worship service of a Christian church and, specifically, the role of the congregation in the receiving of the Word.

The congregation is an assembly of active participants in the drama of the liturgy. They are the focus in worship, in terms of their acts of praise to God. In that sense, they are actors. This, of course, says a great deal about how they go to church, how they participate in worship, how they conduct themselves, how they maintain their reverence, and what they should expect of the sermon. Indeed, it assumes that they know what a sermon in worship should provide. In worship they are truly the body of Christ collectively brought together. They are the people of God coming in God's name to celebrate in praise who God is and, in reverence, who they are. They are hearing their own story as Christians but, more importantly, they are hearing the Christian story recalled. The sermon is a reminder that the story goes on, that it is theirs, and in turn they are urged to keep the memory of Jesus alive in their lives and stories.

Specifically, this may mean a great deal to their lives as Christians. If the sermon has as one reason for being the edification of believers—reminding them of who they are—then the congregation is not responding to a monologue but is responding by becoming articulate believers in their own right. Whatever else preaching does, it should enable laypersons to become articulate in the faith. One might argue that a belief is not a belief until it can be stated, and thereby appropriated. Laypersons hearing their story, being reminded of who they are, can then begin to externalize what they have internalized, and in the "saying" of it, they will have made it their own—and also will have participated in the witnessing of faith to others.

Congregations also can see that as participants in the drama of worship, they are involved in the entire worship event, as well as the clergy, choir, or organ. To see their place visibly as the people of God at worship means that from Prelude to Postlude the attitude is worshipful, and it may call for a more reverent silence than is often prevalent in churches. The "opening exercises" before the sermon are no longer that but are acts of worship in which the people respond to God's grace, and their participation is indeed their entering into the holy of holies. The way they sit, kneel, sing, or participate in responses and hymns should not be as observers or spectators but as actors who are praising God in song, prayer, praise, and response to the Word read and preached. Even the listening can be an act of worship, if they sense that they are before God, hearing the Word. Their listening can be worshipful, an act of praise, and ideally even a dialogue, if they are bringing their response in faith. It is not the preacher they are observing. They, along with the preacher, are acting out their faithfulness before God.

The idea of the preacher as prompter is fruitful for both the preacher and the people. For the preacher, it means he or she is no longer to be considered the "star" of the "show." The preacher is not speaking down to the people, telling them off, embodying the gospel in his or her own person, so that the response to the preacher is response to God or to the faith. As the preacher, he or she is truly the "prompter," whispering the lines—as it were—to the congregation, the lines they should be saying. The preacher reminds them of their history, who they are, whose they are, and what is expected of them—as well as what is expected of the preacher. The preacher does not make up a new gospel, as if it is something they have never heard. Rather, it is a familiar story applied in new ways to their lives in the present context. The churches in the Reformed tradition often place the creed following the sermon. That is certainly appropriate in emphasizing that the sermon is itself in many ways stating the faith of the Christians who are worshiping together.

This stance of the preacher as "prompter" says a great deal about the preacher's understanding of the role of the pulpit. For example, the *ethos* of the preacher as one with authority but not as authoritarian is obvious in such a reunderstanding of the preacher's role. The understanding of the minister as teaching elder, as defined by the former Presbyterian Church, U.S., may be helpful here. It defined teaching elder as not above ruling elders but as set apart by training to do the task of proclamation. This understanding also says something about the language of the pulpit. So many preachers speak imperatively: "you ought," or "you must." No doubt there are times for that, but to understand preaching as "prompting" is to suggest that preaching is more the indicative mood than the imperative. Though in the material on language this point will again be emphasized, it is worth noting that a statement such as Paul's to the Ephesians, "you are no longer strangers and sojourners, but you are fellow citizens with the saints and members of the household of God" (2:19) has the advantage of stating and telling, not scolding and judging, as the regular diet of preaching. No one should believe that the indicative eliminates the prophetic. On the contrary, to remind persons of who they are, what their history is, and what God expects of them can bring judgment as easily as solace. We have often said that the pastoral prayer is a priestly function, lifting up the needs of the people to God, and the sermon is speaking on behalf of God to the people. Perhaps so, but the preacher speaking on behalf of God is not to bring news that is unknown to the Christians at worship. It is a story they have heard, and to be reminded of it can bring again the good news and can also remind us of our faithlessness in living up to that saving Word.

One of the most interesting things that the preacher can do is to radiate some excitement to the people about the Christian story. It might be argued that one of the problems with the church today is not that preachers do not preach the gospel or challenge the congregation to action but that as preachers we simply bore people. In visiting a large church a few years ago, I noticed that as soon as the sermon began a man, sitting in the pew in front of me, pulled out a small instruction book on golf and began practicing golf swings in his lap while the preacher droned on through the sermon. I pondered what the preacher would think if he knew what was happening in the pews. The boredom is not always due to the need for better communication techniques or training, nor is it due to the congregation's conditioned responses to the excitement of television. The bottom line in many cases is that the preacher is either not sold on what he or she has to give or is simply bored with it. The incarnation, to give but one example, is a terribly exciting idea when it is contemplated, but pulpits can dampen enthusiasm even for the idea that God was in a baby. To take Søren Kierkegaard seriously, then, means not only the reordering of many congregations' ideas but perhaps an even more radical transformation for the preacher.

The central figure in the drama of liturgy is, of course, God. Both the congregation and preacher are allied in acknowledging this premise and are copartners in bringing themselves to worship. Whether it is praise or prayer, offering of money or self, sermon or sacrament, the object of the worship experience is crystal clear. God is both the subject and the object. We are reminded of God's grace, and worship is a response to that grace. We worship in praise, go beyond ourselves in awe, and are reminded of the grace within us as humans. Whether or not we use terms such as Kierkegaard used, that God is the audience—the Critic-Judge, it is clear that the preacher and congregation are coming together as actors in the drama of worshiping God.

Since the key focus of this chapter is the congregation, we need to look more in depth at its role in the sermon process. In the Kierkegaard analogy we have already seen its indispensable place in the worship event. It seems incredible that the congregation is assumed, but unfortunately for many preachers, the congregation becomes almost a nonfactor. Though there are undoubtedly many reasons for this—all the way from not thinking about it at all to simply assuming there will be a congregation—one of the chief reasons is that preachers tend to be more subjective than objective in terms of the congregation.[1] By subjective is meant the temptation to think of one's theme or self, irrespective of the congregation. Objective in this sense does not mean considering the congregation an object but rather that the preacher stands outside self and subject to consider those who are receiving the message. In communication we know that the sender needs a receiver, else communication does not take place. The same for the sermon. It is not some gnostic sacrament that has efficacy apart from a congregation. As we have seen, the congregation and the preacher are joined together in worship as actors before God. They are not separate entities.

The same is true for the sermon. The congregation is an indispensable element of the preaching event itself.[2] Fred Craddock quotes Manfred Mezger that "an opera may be right and valid without an audience, but a service of the Word is a call, and a call is meaningless without a hearer."[3] That is the theme both of communication and communion.

The ignoring of the congregation is not always conscious. At the same time, the consideration of the congregation is not always conscious, either. A good minister-pastor will obviously carry into the study the concerns and needs of his or her particular church, his or her particular people. That kind of eisegesis is always involved in good preaching and, indeed, is necessary to good preaching. Thus, an effective pastor may be carrying the persons into the study, bringing text and people together. Stories are also told of sensitive preachers who consciously identify people specifically and how their needs are met in a particular sermon. In earlier times, a story is told of a preacher who on Saturday went out into the empty church and sat in different places, attempting to visualize how the sermon would affect this one or that. The intent is not to "trim the sails" of a sermon to suit the biases and prejudices of the people but to identify with their needs and to see if the sermon will be spraying the universe with rhetoric or will be a Word through words to specific worshipers.

Historically, there has been a great deal more concern with congregations than one would think. In the early church, the earliest preaching was missionary preaching to the pagans or the unchurched. This point is the one Dodd makes by delineating kerygmatic preaching in the New Testament and suggesting that such preaching (e.g., Peter's sermons in Acts) was normative for the early church. In his terms it can be construed as the definition of preaching itself. Later, as the church grew and became more regularized, preaching had different functions. The variety was due to the status of the people responding to the gospel message. There was still the preaching to the pagans or the unchurched, so-called missionary preaching. For those who had become Christians, the newly baptized, there was catechetical preaching—a type that was for edifying the new believers and giving them instruction in the faith. Finally, there were post-baptized Christians who received communion, and the sermon in that context was the homily.[4] Interestingly enough, in St. Augustine's time, all of the above would be in the same church. There was a place for the unchurched, a section for the catechumens, and then those who would receive the elements as full-fledged members of Christ's body were seated in their own section. Sometimes the former two groups were dismissed entirely.[5] Though modern congregations are not so rigidly codified, it is wrong to assume that even our typical Sunday morning services have homogenized congregations. Certainly, and somewhat unfortunately, members do congregate according to geography, class, political leanings—often more sociologically united than theologically. Still, James Seller's book, *The Outsider and the Word of God*,[6] even though written some years ago, reminds us that many of the true outsiders are in the congregation, and conversely, many of the real insiders are outside the walls of the church all together.

In our day, even the most unified congregation in a typical church with theological, political, and sociological closeness is still a dynamic, changing, unpredictable, and individualistic group. It is for these reasons that the preacher must go beyond even the apparent unity of his or her members, and beyond what is imagined to be the closeness engendered in worship, as the group is brought together to worship God. One needs to go beyond even the assumptions that as pastors we "know" our people and their needs. The effective preacher will need to drop the subjective mode of ignoring the congregation, as the sermon is prepared around the lectionary, the text, and the preacher's own interests. As we have seen, such a stance is an extension of one's concern, not only pastorally, but as a person who is specifically interested in "going the second mile" in communing (or communicating) with the congregation. That is not only both a pastoral and a theological concern; it is a communicative one as well, recognizing that the former, no matter how much engendered by good will, is not enough in our electronic age.

One will need to analyze the congregation specifically before one preaches. *Analyze*, though it sounds clinical and rationalistic, can be construed as being sensitive to those in the pews. We have seen that a strong pastor may be doing this week by week unconsciously. But, even the sensitive pastor will need to give attention to the congregation's predisposition from time to time. The congregation changes from week to week in many instances. Too, the text, subject, or theme may in itself change the congregation from what it might have been the Sunday before. A sermon on self-denial in Lent may create a different mind-set in the congregation than the next Sunday's sermon on the dangers of the arms race does. One way, then, of looking directly at the congregation is to consider the response sought from them. The question, "what do I want my congregation to do as a response to this sermon?" is a good beginning for an in-depth probing of the congregation. To the uninitiated this might sound like manipulation, but to the caring pastor it means sensitivity to the people who have been entrusted to his or her care. The so-called evangelist has always been concerned with response. To the one who proceeds on the assumption that the gospel presents a claim and there must be a response, it is natural to assume that the response sought is "a coming to the altar" or some other variation of that traditional action.

At one level, probing the congregation is disarmingly simple. A preacher knows generally that the people, for example, are rural, mid-westerners, generally Republicans, or that they are urban, blue-collar, industrial, unionized, workers, Democrats. However, even within such categories, people differ—no congregation can be seen just as a whole. The psychological makeup is different within individuals. Even within a family, one person may be buoyant and another morose. Grief, be-reavement, the loss of a job, a promotion, a new job, or a forthcoming marriage can change an individual almost overnight. Such sensitivity by the pastor not only makes him or her more effective in the study as a counselor but such sensitivity is just as imperative in the pulpit. Of course, the preacher cannot meet everyone's needs from the pulpit every Sunday. However, the mandate is clear. Those people in that congregation cannot be taken for granted. There may be one level where it is apparent that the generalizations about the group may be valid, but there are deeper levels in individuals and congregations which must be understood, if the preacher is to be effective—not alone as a pastor—but also as a preacher.

There are several factors which can affect the congregation and the preacher as well, which might be called the context of the preaching event. Many preachers are unaware that such things as the physical set-ting have an effect on the preaching of the sermon or the hearing of the congregation.[7] Take, for example, the seating of the congregation. One could, without a great deal of thought, ruin an effective sermon by reseating the congregation. If the congregation is smaller than a large sanctuary warrants, this usually leaves front pews vacant. Stragglers are often in a practically unused balcony, and some persons may sit in a back section under the shadow of the balcony. Thus, the preacher may be straining and having a difficult time in communicating without really knowing the problem. What is at stake here is the dispersal of the congregation into separate entities without the feeling of togetherness which can occur in a true congregation. Communication theorists would speak of the importance of a psychological crowd. There is a correlation between physical closeness and psychological closeness, as we know if we attend political rallies, basketball games, or musical events. That same phenomenon is present in church, especially since we are brought together with a similar purpose in worship. Our being together is both physical and spiritual. Fracturing the physical body by distances fractures the spiritual closeness. We are not called upon to build "psychological crowds," but we can take steps to bring our people together. To take but one example, if a congregational setting is as described above, then keeping the balcony closed, having ushers give out bulletins down the aisle away from the overhanging balconies, and even roping off the last few pews are the kinds of things that might be done (with representative congregational help) to bring the worshipers into closer proximity with one another. That offers an atmosphere for physical and spiritual unity.

Even a public address system can wreak havoc in separating the preacher from the congregation. The people may be getting an amplified sound from a disembodied voice. Larger churches are not the only ones with this problem; small rural churches often end up with a system given by someone who is hard of hearing and too proud to move up in the pews, and/or too vain to get a hearing aid. For the preacher, it often encourages sloppy enunciation, lack of projection, and bad habits of articulation. In many cases, public address systems are used when not needed. In other instances, where it is imperative because of size or acoustics, a sound engineer should be consulted before installing mechanized amplification.

What is said about the physical setting could also be duplicated in relation to lighting, the chancel furniture, and even the worship service itself. All have bearing on the congregation and its response to preaching, as well as its participation. A spotlight on the pulpit and the lowering of lights in the congregation when the sermon begins says something about the preacher's ego and ethos and the congregation's place in the preaching event as a joint enterprise. The preacher's size in relation to the chancel furniture (i.e., pulpit, lectern) can even affect the congregation. Too tall for a short pulpit, too short for a tall lectern, too boxed in by the pulpit—all can be imperceptible factors in the congregation's relation to the sermon. The arrangement of the worship service and where items come can also be a problem. Arrangement for audience effect should never govern a worship service or take precedence over liturgy, theology, and worship, but a casual or unthought-through service can work to the detriment of the rapport with the congregation. To give but one example, some of us feel strongly that an anthem before the sermon does not help the unity of the congregation before the preacher speaks. It is an item without congregational participation, and unless the choir is terribly effective, minds wander, attention is lost, and the crowd which may have been unified throughout the service has had that unity dissipated. If the choir is strong, then the preacher's introduction may be anticlimactic in changing the mood or refocusing the attention. A hymn before the sermon, the Scripture, or a creed recited together are some of the ways the congregation can be involved, often on their feet, becoming more of a unified group as the sermon begins.

The size of the congregation can change the ethos of a congregation and force the preacher to enter into a different dynamic than that for which he or she prepared. The predominant age of the congregation, dominance of one sex over another, prevailing occupation, or educational background are all factors that a sensitive preacher will need to take into account as he or she "reads" the congregation. Certainly we are not referring to "special pleading" and adopting the biases and prejudicial biases of a given community. *Adopting* and *adapting to* are quite different in intent and result.[8]

Perhaps more familiar to us in our day are the psychological categories of personalities with which we deal often in pastoral counseling. Without attempting to enter into that area in any exhaustible way, it is important to remember that the same needs of persons in the counseling setting are operative also in the congregation on Sunday morning. The preacher who is concerned with these needs is the preacher who is not only vitally interested in his or her people as human beings but is also a minister who is carrying those needs into his or her sermon preparation and pulpit presentation. It is not necessary here to enunciate the many needs that persons bring to a speech situation. There are those who theologically affirm that the basic drive of humans is original sin or *hubris*. In any event, whether called theological or not, humans do have egos of which preachers need to be aware. Those egos can go all the way from thinking too highly of oneself to deprecating one's humanness. All of us are wrestling with the fragile ego. Suffice it to say that the skills a pastor has as a counselor are at work in a sensitive preacher's sermons, first of all in his or her concern for the congregation but also in the effectiveness of the sermon's reception.[9]

If sensitivity to the concerns and needs of a congregation is important week by week, there is one area where such a concern is imperative. For the preacher who addresses on controversial issues, a clear reading of the congregation in light of the theme of that sermon will be absolutely necessary. Some communication theorists who study crowd behavior affirm that audiences can be classified. For example, there are believing audiences, doubting audiences, hostile audiences, and indifferent audiences. Further, the material presented to these audiences will vary in amount and placement. Many of these so-called experts label the religious audience a "believing" one. By this is meant that the congregation is predisposed to religion, faith, and even the preacher's point of view. For such a group, the materials used in a "sermon" would be heavy on experience (preacher's, the story, the people's) to intensify their beliefs, authority (Scripture, tradition, and the preacher's), and reason—all in that order. However, for a doubting audience (a preacher on a secular college campus), one would use reason first, then authority (of self and others), and finally experience (to keep up interest). The hostile audience (proposing nuclear disarmament in front of an American Legion convention) would need authority (of the speaker and of other accepted sources), reason, and then experience. Apathetic or indifferent audiences usually become one of the three above when their interests are aroused.

Whatever may be the accuracy of such communicative analyses of audiences, this much is clear for congregations. A so-called believing audience can become a hostile one when the preacher comes to controversial subjects, either in theological/biblical or social areas. The preacher who assumes a congregation is a static entity will be rudely awakened when moving into controversial areas, and the wise preacher will attempt to understand the people's predispositions and the ways he or she might present the material to get an effective hearing. Not dealing with the issue at all is not what we are suggesting. How does one deal responsibly with controversy, maintain one's integrity, and get a hearing, if not agreement? Understanding the congregation is absolutely basic. Most important is undoubtedly the *ethos* of the preacher. Most people are more hostile to a person's ideas than to the person. If the preacher is a good pastor, accepted and loved by the congregation, then it is possible to move into sensitive areas and be heard—often sympathetically. The material used would also be decisive. The more controversial the sermon theme, the more expository the sermon. Some consider that approach normative for all preaching, but it has particular force in controversial preaching. And finally, knowing the congregation will enable the pastor to present the volatile material sensitively without shutting ears or losing his or her own integrity.

The congregation is the warp and woof of the preaching event. The preacher who seeks to be persuasive "knows his sheep and is known by them" (see John 10:14). He or she desires to know them, not for manipulation, not even to motivate them to a specific response necessarily but simply to communicate with them. In knowing their needs, the preacher can combine the affective and the cognitive in the preaching experience, thereby being both convincing and moving.

10

The Sermon Event: Hearing

One of the most audible, visual, and vital aspects of the incarnational understanding of proclamation is the language used in preaching. We have gone all the way from a correct, formal style to a complete depreciation of language and style—both spoken and written. The former suggests to many the florid use of language—long, involved sentences, conscious alliteration, and "pretty" prose. The latter depreciates style in language, often opting for the staccato oral language reminiscent of a telegram. Words, however, are the only means we have for clothing our ideas, and care with them takes the same dedication that one would have with exegesis, clarity, form, delivery, and even the gospel itself. Fred Craddock[1] reminds us that the only words we have are human words. If so, then that which encases the message may be decisive in its receptivity.

St. Augustine,[2] in one of the earliest of Christian rhetorics, spoke of the importance of style. For him, the eloquent person speaks in such a way as to teach, delight, and move. Quoting Cicero, he suggested that one can speak of small things in a subdued manner, moderate things in a temperate manner, and grand things in a grand manner. It was his intention to relate the latter three styles to the former purposes of eloquence. It is interesting to note, however, that eloquence for Augustine was not prized above clarity. "The speaker should not consider the eloquence of his teaching but the clarity of it."[3] In our day we are undoubtedly less indebted to St. Augustine than we are to Ernest Hemingway. Nevertheless, we neglect style at our peril, at least in regard to the language we use in transmitting the gospel.

On the first level is the concern for grammar. Certainly, a split infinitive, a dangling participle, or a sentence ending with a preposition cannot be considered a capital offense. At the same time, preachers who spend their lives with words as "the tools of their trade" should be able to speak correctly. Though there are areas of debate in regard to usage, distinctions can be made between slang and colloquial speech, blatant incorrectness and normative usage, illiteracy and regional dialects. The preacher who says that he has a secret but "it is just between you and *I*" or that "the church has given a nice present to Helen and *I*" is hindering the receptivity of the message. The person who cannot straighten out the difference between *lie* and *lay* in the pulpit offends congregations, often without knowing it, but offends, just the same. We should not try to please every fastidious grammarian who may be occupying a pew in the church, but correct usage seems to be a minimal requirement for the one who will be spending an entire lifetime using words and language. As we saw in connection with ethos, competence is as important as integrity and good will. One's use of the language is as integral to the congregation's perception of the preacher's competence as is preparation, clarity, ideas, or biblical and theological faithfulness.

Good usage also affects clarity. As we have seen, clarity of ideas is important for a meaningful gospel. So, too, is clarity decisive in oral expression and language usage. Even St. Augustine, who prized style highly, reminds us that clarity ranks higher than eloquence. Pablo Casals, in speaking of a teacher who sat beside him at the piano and admonished him to play in the language of everybody, remembered the advice as a profound utterance for the purpose of art in general. "What purpose, indeed, can music—or any form of art—serve if it does not speak in a language that all can understand?"[4] What is true for music and other art forms is no less true for the preaching of the pulpit.

Beyond clarity and correct usage, though, one of the most important questions is how can we speak of the holy in earthy terms? In one sense, we spend our lives trying to make the unknown known, the divine human, the abstract concrete, and the general specific. Inheriting biblical and theological categories and language, we are eternally engaged in the attempt to de- or remythologize them into everyday usage, without either trivializing the language or going through a process of theological reductionism. The most obvious way we do that is by using analogy, metaphor, simile, or tropes. The rhetorical and philological niceties are not the primary concern of the preacher, but a grasp of the importance of existentializing the faith into arresting forms of contemporaneity is the challenge for all preachers. Through the ages, Christians all the way from biblical translators to theologians to parish ministers struggle to repossess the faith for the present. Luther is but one of an endless line of such Christians who not only translated the Bible into the language of the people but preached in the same way; thus, it is no wonder that the common people heard him gladly.

As preachers, we need to trust our own ability to state our ideas correctly, interestingly, pictorially, and even excitingly. Most preachers tend to think of using language arrestingly as illustrations; hence, the temptation to buy books that will serve up secondhand stories for every theme. These helps shortcut the preacher's awareness of his or her own personal possession, the ability to use language in a unique and creative way. Edwin Newman concludes an article on the demise of language usage by declaring, "The language belongs to all of us. We have no more valuable possession."[5] We have already seen the importance of words as the custodians and transmitters of the Word. One of the personal treasures each preacher possesses is the ability to use words in a way no one else can duplicate. This does not mean glibness or using words to control, divide, or label. Words are potent and must be seen for the power inherent within them. Dr. Jack L. Stotts, in a charge to Dr. Don M. Wardlaw as a Professor of Preaching and Worship, made perceptive comments on the importance of words.

> . . . teach us so to speak and to be that our words will serve the purpose of a Word whose work and calling was reconciliation of the whole creation.
> That is, allow that Word to wrestle with you so that all your and our words are open to repentance and reformulation. Then we will understand that when we dance before the Lord it is always the dance of a cripple; that when we speak it is always the stutterings of imprecision; that when we worship it is always a failed drama. Yet dance we may. Speak we can. And worship we must. For we are by God's grace ourselves articulations of the Word by the power of the Spirit. . . . Help us to love and therefore to wrestle with the Word and the words.[6]

If we are ourselves articulations of the Word, then we have been given the gift to articulate words as a response. Our task is to accept the Word and incarnationally place it in our words. The creative wrestling with the faith on the one hand and our own vocabularies on the other can comprise both the agony and ecstasy of preaching. But, we must trust ourselves to do it, as we have been trusted. A sermon by a seminary student reveals the power of putting things in one's own words. In a sermon on the theme of God's searching us rather than our searching God, the preacher said:

> We are trained to think God chooses us because of who we are, but we are called to believe that God chooses us in spite of who we are. . . . God does not ask us to demand *more of* ourselves; God asks us to demand *less for* ourselves. . . . To imagine that Jacob is out searching for God is like imagining that the mouse is searching for the cat. . . . While the world glories in more and more, Christ exults in less and less.[7]

These excerpts are examples to show that a conscientious preacher can use his or her own vocabulary to carry the message arrestingly and indeed paint pictures. Long illustrations need not be inserted, especially if the style of the preacher itself can make the material vivid. Pictures can be drawn and painted with one's own vocabulary, if the preacher takes the time to work with the style which uniquely belongs to him or her.

In spite of the cautions noted, illustrations are certainly a valid way of using language to confirm the Word. Books are available which provide illustrations as well as books which treat illustrations and their nature and use in some detail. For our purposes, a few highlights will suffice as the basic theory for the use of illustrations. Most basic is the obvious. Illustrations should lead to the point. If the illustration is remembered but not the idea illustrated, then it has failed. Illustrations should flow outwardly from the point, not be superimposed so as to obscure or overpower the point being made. Many sermons are like Christmas trees, decorated with illustrations by the preacher who stands off and throws baubles and tinsel at the tree, as if the decoration is more important than the tree. Illustrations grow out of the idea seeking a form, not vice versa.

Another quality of illustrating that can be highlighted is the universal nature of effective illustrations. There are areas which touch upon the common experiences of persons everywhere. Love, music, and suffering are only three instances of materials which touch many people, if the illustrations can reflect such qualities. To affirm this negates the belief that only certain kinds of illustrations can be used here or there, because the congregation is rural or because it is urban. If a theme is on suffering, then whether the example comes from Elmira, New York, or Ethiopia, Africa, the illustration could be effective. If the preacher is speaking of love, the illustration could be a quotation from a philosopher as well as an example from the parish. There might be more "closeness" with the one or the other, but the universality of the example can transcend time and space.

A comparison with literature can be apt at this point. A writer who is regional is one who knows what he or she is closest to and has a "feel" for the territory. However, if one only writes about the area in a provincial way, he or she becomes a special pleader and is trapped by the region. A regional writer, however, who writes about universal themes not only is nurtured by the native soil but has transcended it to write for persons everywhere. Many examples could be given. Frost's poetry transcends New England because his themes are human ones. The same could be said for Southern writers such as Flannery O'Connor, Eudora Welty, Robert Penn Warren, and William Faulkner. The region nourishes them but does not trap them.

One aspect of illustration needs mentioning, if only negatively. "Canned" illustrations which come from books of illustrations or which make the rounds after a preachers' conference are often lifeless, smell of paste, scissors, and old files. They sound secondhand because they are. However, they are often told as if the incidents described happened to each preacher. The lack of spontaneity and the falsity of the illustration make it seem lifeless when placed alongside an incident which the preacher discovered on his or her own. The preacher should cultivate the kinds of reading habits that will allow wide-ranging experience through books. Varying cultural experiences offer opportunities to discover for oneself the joy of coming across material that can be personally possessed, and used as sermon illustrations.

Perhaps the most important thing to be said in regard to illustrations addresses the use of the personal. The place of the personal, one's own story, and the place of autobiography are held in high regard at the present time. However, one who looks at this mode of discourse should do so with some caution in terms of confidence. Many good things can be said about the use of the personal, but there are also pathologies in overinvolving the ego in the preaching event. Certainly, if one can vivify the gospel message in one's own experience or can embody the point in some incident close to one's life, then the material will have more spontaneity, will dramatize the gospel in a most personal way, and can be more existential. Such a view fits in with the ethos of the preacher's presence being important in the event, as well as buttressing the incarnational aspects of preaching. Thomas Oden states the importance of the personal story.

> Admittedly one's own personal story is the lens through which the larger Christian story is seen. But *it is not just private experience that deserves to be reported*. . . . You must risk telling your own story, not as an end in itself, but rather as a sharply focused lens *through which the whole Christian story is refracted* (italics mine).[8]

This comment shows the importance and the danger of the autobiographical story. Certainly the preacher's person is highly involved in proclamation in a way that is not present in other speech occasions. The preacher's ethos and the embodying of the word are integral to the preaching event. At the same time Oden's cautions are often overlooked, and the preacher, unfortunately, embarks on an autobiographical excursion, unconsciously preaching not Christ but self. A preacher can reveal a counseling situation—a danger in itself in relation to ethos—in which he or she unwittingly becomes the hero. Or a preacher may involve, without prior clearance, his or her family and friends in the sermon, which may be a cause for embarrassment. Ethos is not the same as egotism, and the wise preacher will take care to walk gingerly between these two poles.

Of course, the whole issue of the personal illustration and the role of autobiography is much larger than simply how to illustrate a sermon. It raises the much larger and extremely important area of story itself as a form of sermonic discourse. As we have seen from Oden's statement, we are advised as Christian preachers to risk telling our own story because it is the lens through which the whole Christian story is refracted. Story, personal and otherwise, has a great emphasis in our present day. The narrative, or story, becomes a means of telling the gospel. It reminds us of the Story by telling a story. In fact, it is affirmed that the story is the grammar of theological discourse. It combines events and people together. The story may not be making points; it is the point. Often the paradigm for the story form is attributed to Jesus, who spoke in parables; therefore, Jesus' form of discourse itself becomes the form that we should trust as we tell our story of the Christian faith.

Without negating the importance of story and narrative as forms of discourse or as ways of presenting the Christian story, some cautions need to be raised for the use of the personal story as the "lens" for the Christian story. We have already seen the seductive way the personal may lead the preacher into self-aggrandizement. More important, the preacher's personal story may be worthless unless it points to or illuminates *the Story*. Preachers should not assume that their stories embrace the entire gamut of the Christian faith. To assume that one's experiences encompass the Christian story, that they are universal, or that they are even always interesting to someone else, invests the preacher with an omnicompetence that borders on presumptuousness. Sam Keen, in an otherwise excellent and creative book, *To a Dancing God*,[9] tells the story of his relationship with his father, and presumably this has a lesson for us as Christians. After reading the tender incident, I had to admit that his story did not tell me a thing about my relationship with either my earthly father or my heavenly one, and so I was distanced from both his story and the insight. I became a spectator, not a participant, in the story event. The question for the preacher becomes: does my story enhance the Story?

A further caution comes in the theological area. If Jesus in speaking in parables becomes the paradigm for our use of narrative, story, parable, are we preachers making a theological statement as well as a literary one? For some the answer is obviously *yes*. The focus is on Jesus as teacher, preacher, parable maker. Is such a focus, however, running the risk of theological reductionism? Can Jesus' person and work be truncated? Can we separate his human life and teachings from the claims that the church has made about him in the cross/resurrection event? Those who root the story form in the parabolic teachings of Jesus are also making a theological statement as to the theological nature of Jesus himself.

A final caution as to the use of story comes at the point of aesthetics. The preacher who embraces narrative is often vitally interested in literature, theater, music, and other art expressions which provide form and often content for storytelling. Such cultural manifestations are vital to clergy for many reasons, including broadening the sensitivities, providing source materials, and giving the preacher insight into culture itself. However, many assume a creative bent and training many preachers do not have. It could be possible that it is more difficult for a working pastor to master aesthetics than dogmatics or exegesis. The reservation is simply that the entire realm of narrative, parable, and story is opening up important creative areas for the preacher, but we ought to remember that such a realm will be affected by one's own background, training, and interest. In short, some will handle creativity more easily than others in this area, just as in other fields.

If the story form has some problems as well as advantages, there is certainly nothing negative about the use of narrative itself. We have alluded to the fact that analogically may be the only way humans have of speaking of the divine. For its own sake, however, preaching becomes more holistic, existential, and event-like if the discourse is multi-leveled, affective/cognitive, and dramatic. Moving from the didactic to the pictorial enhances both the communication of the gospel by the preacher and the reception by the congregation. Janice Huie emphasizes the importance of metaphor in this way:

> By metaphorical preaching I mean communicating the gospel through the
> use of story, image, and poetry. . . . Metaphor can enable us to transcend a
> prosaic style of preaching, which frequently reduces both men and women
> to heads without hearts, minds without spirits. Metaphor is participatory
> rather than authoritarian. It implies a partnership between preacher and
> congregation in which the preachers speak *for, with,* and *from* the people
> rather than *to* people. Metaphor invites the whole people of God to envi-
> sion and live in the new creation.[10]

It is this holistic way of communicating, plus the necessity to talk of
God in analogical language, that serves to make discourse in the pulpit
move from the didactic to the dramatic. The ways to do that are myriad, and a preacher is only bound by his or her creativity and imagination. Though the sermon is rightly one's own creation, there are models
aplenty which can spark our imagination, not in the sense of copying
examples as much as whetting our appetites to do the same kinds of
things. A preacher whose reading, for example, is wide-ranging will
have a multitude of areas in which to find reflected imaginative ways of
seeing God's work in the world. C. S. Lewis, to name but one, has an
uncanny knack for using analogical examples to make clear the way he
sees the divine in the human. Though his theological views do not appeal to all Christians, his creative use of figurative language should.

First of all, consider Lewis' understanding of metaphor:

> . . . it is a serious mistake to think that metaphor is an optional thing which
> poets and orators may put into their work as a decoration and plain speak-
> ers can do without. The truth is that if we are going to talk at all about
> things which are not perceived by the senses, we are forced to use language
> metaphorically. Books on psychology or economics or politics are as con-
> tinuously metaphorical as books of poetry or devotion. There is no other
> way of talking, as every philologist is aware.[11]

He notes further that in an endeavor to get rid of traditional religious concepts and language, we succeed only in substituting other
figures. He states that in order to escape anthropomorphic images we
often come up with other images even less helpful. He tells of a person
who says, "I don't believe in a personal God, but I do believe in a
great spiritual force." *Force*, Lewis points out, creates all kinds of
images about winds and tides and electricity and gravitation. He also
tells of the person who says, "I don't believe in a personal God, but I
do believe we are all part of one great Being which moves and works

through us all." This exchanges the image of a fatherly and royal-looking man for the image of some widely extended gas or fluid. He then tells of knowing a young woman brought up by parents to think of God as a perfect "substance," and she confessed later that this had led her to think of God as a vast tapioca pudding.[12]

Still, we use metaphorical language, perhaps even at the risk of theological reductionism, or we use images which are not adequate for the divine. We keep on because our language is what we use to transmit the gospel. It would probably be better for a preacher to fall on his or her face trying to make God alive in the minds and hearts of the congregation than to speak didactically and dismally in theologically abstract terms. Lewis' theory can be illustrated in multiform ways in his writings. In one place he speaks of the Christian way as being both easier and harder.

> Christ says, "Give me All. I don't want so much of your time and so much of your money and so much of your work: I want You. I have not come to torment your natural self, but to kill it. No half-measures are any good. I don't want to cut off a branch here and a branch there, I want to have the whole tree down. I don't want to drill the tooth, or crown it, or stop it, but to have it out. Hand over the whole natural self, all the desires which you think innocent as well as the ones you think wicked—the whole outfit. I will give you a new self instead. In fact, I will give you Myself: my own will shall become yours."[13]

> If I'm a field that contains nothing but grass-seed, I can't produce wheat. Cutting the grass may keep it short: but I shall still produce grass and no wheat. If I want to produce wheat, the change must go deeper than the surface. I must be ploughed up and re-sown.[14]

One of the most important aspects of language in our day is the whole area of inclusive language. Though this controversial area has ramifications for biblical study, hymnology, and history of doctrine, it also has particular impact on the pulpit. The pulpit is visual, ever-present, and the public place where Christian discourse and language are on display. Though it is not the intention here to give full-blown attention to that difficult and intriguing subject, principles are at work which affect preaching quite decisively. Some biblical scholars are cautious about preachers changing biblical texts without knowing the biblical languages, though in many instances changes made by scholars can often aid inclusiveness. Debatable areas exist in theology in regard to uncritical changing of exclusive language, not the least of which is theological reductionism. And, hymnologists will wince when texts are changed without regard to rhyme, poetry, or musical adaptation. Some wonder why time should be spent in attempting to redo ancient hymns when time might be spent in writing new hymns for our day. Some people are offended grammatically if language is changed and sentences end up either incorrect or awkward so as to call attention to the change. In all of these instances, changes can, do, and should occur.

The difficulties should in no way hinder the attempt to make the faith and the language of faith inclusive. When a preacher stands in the pulpit to preach, he or she has no excuse not to be inclusive in every way. The language we use to tell the story or preach the gospel rests in our hands. It is not handed down or secondhand. It is ours. There are at least two ways that the preacher can manifest inclusiveness. First, in ideas and illustrations. Second, in language itself. In terms of God, for instance, "Father" is certainly a hallowed symbol for God, but it is by no means the only image. Any anthropomorphic designation will fall short of encompassing the God concept, whether male or female. God does not have to be wholly other to be beyond our language and vocabularies. All designations fail, but in using our limited language we certainly do not need to be locked into only male terminology. The parent God, for example, can express the closeness of the Divine without the usual "Father" or "God he. . . ." As we saw in metaphorical language, we run the risk of diminishing the Divine in our limited language, but we must take the risk in regard to seeing God as God of all.

In the case of illustration, we have even more choice and freedom to be inclusive. Most male preachers are unaware of the persistent tendencies to use male examples in their illustrations and even in their use of biblical materials. Occasionally Mary and Martha do get mentioned. Yet, even given the hierarchal and male dominance in the Bible, hosts of texts and incidents are present which play up the role of women as well as men. Abraham and Sarah, for example, can be seen together. A consciousness-raising in this regard can uncover a veritable gold mine of persons to represent a feminine point of view. What is true for the Bible is true for church history. Our so-called Church Fathers have been accompanied through the ages by Church Mothers. The saints have been of both sexes, and we ignore them not only to the detriment of inclusiveness but even more important to the richness of the faith itself. In our contemporary Christian scene the same is true. Preachers often neglect women as subjects of the illustrative material. For every Mother Theresa example, probably ten examples are males. Preachers can become much more sensitive in regard to the examples they use, which often exclude more than half of their congregations.

And, finally, in regard to language, we do have complete control over our own speech and language in the pulpit. Our own discourse is ours, and no reason whatsoever is available as to why we cannot always be inclusive in our speaking. We can use our preaching style to include all of those who sit before us. That is not a question of theology or biblical faithfulness: it is the question of making our communication truly communion, which is the requirement for all of our Christian discourse.

11

Language That
Serves God

Though our concern here is with the preaching office, it is imperative to remind ourselves that preaching takes place in a context. We
have long bemoaned the unfortunate separation between preaching and
worship manifested in some of the Protestant traditions where the sermon was the entire focus and the worship around it was either considered "opening exercises" or designed merely to enhance the sermon—
and often the preacher. Surely enough has been written to demonstrate
the fact that word and worship are inseparable. Though worship, *per
se*, is not our primary concern, it should be emphasized strongly that
the sermon is an act of worship. One way to state it would be that the
entire service of worship is the preaching event or that the sermon
could be considered a specific act of worship, similar to reciting a
creed—the church confessing its faith.

The long-held shibboleth that assumed that the Protestant tradition has emphasized preaching and the Catholic one liturgy has by this time surely been dealt with adequately. Though there may have been ebbing and flowing in the history of the church, the early church developed the preaching office, and one need only review the fourth century to see the importance of the act of preaching for the historic Christian church. It is also a denigration of the Protestant tradition to assume that liturgy and worship were neglected by all who called themselves Protestants. In modern times, the welding of the two has received emphasis not only by biblical scholars of both traditions preceding Vatican II but also by the widespread use of the lectionary as a preaching and worship instrument by a host of churches which spans all sects and denominations, Catholic and Protestant.

The lectionary causes difficulties for some denominations and preachers. American preachers tend to be "topical" in their preaching, and thus the lectionary either gets in the way or else they end up with a schizophrenic sermon—a topic at war with the text. Others come from traditions which eschew the lectionary as being too formal or too liturgical—not fitting in with the polity of their tradition. Though most preachers use a "lectionary," the prescribed texts seem rigid and too prescriptive to fit their entire preaching schedule. Further, advocates of lectionary preaching often have been rigid in their insistence that all must preach from the lectionary, thereby imparting their own traditions or perspectives to every Christian preacher.

One way to look at the lectionary is to divest it of its liturgical and theological arguments. Of course, those are important, but their weight will vary due to differences in ecclesiology and polity. Pragmatically, however, the working preacher can incorporate the lectionary into the week's work, regardless of polity or theology. Though perhaps topical by nature and training, most preachers will be working with Scripture devotionally, if nothing else. The transition to use of the lectionary as an aid in preaching, among other things, can be both easy and fruitful. It also helps to realize that the lectionary is not sacred. It is not on the level of Holy Scripture in the Christian tradition; thus, it can be seen not only in the liturgical sense, but also homiletically, as an ordered way to develop sermons throughout the Christian year. The lectionary is a resource for developing sermons around the great festivals of the Christian year. These Scriptures scheduled through the Christian year can be seen as the story of our faith, the drama of the gospel, covering the sweep of Christian doctrine.

The lectionary does some specific things for the preacher.[1] First, it provides ideas from which to preach. Each week the lectionary presents "fields to plow in," and though they may not always be fruitful at first glance, the texts will often provide a word, if the task is not given up too soon. Skimming through the lessons for a "quick fix" is not the listening and struggling that preaching involves. Since we do not go to Scriptures *de novo*, part of the struggle involves bringing to the study the needs of the people. The spark that ignites a sermon may occur when the needs of the congregation cross a word that comes from the text. In providing a constant source of ideas, the lesson relieves the preacher of the frantic search that often takes place in the pursuit of sermons. It can be a relief to avoid jumping around all week like a grasshopper with the St. Vitus dance, looking for topics here and there. Many preachers seek sermons from everything they read, from comic strips to magazines, to movies they see, to counseling sessions they have, and even to TV programs. As the week wanes, and the sermon is not underway, the preacher often approaches panic. The lectionary can reduce this frenetic pace of the pastor in the search of sermon topics as well as help focus the work of the preacher.

Similarly, the lectionary saves the preacher from trying to preach a "great" sermon each Sunday. Many times the preacher will try to "top" last Sunday's message. If one preaches what one considers to be an effective sermon, then it is natural to do at least as well, or better, the next time. The lectionary may remind us that we are unfolding Scripture as pastors, and we are not to strive for oratorical pyrotechnics. It was Bultmann who reminded us that we are not called to be great but to be faithful.[2] The lectionary reminds us of the faithfulness of the expositor of the Christian message.

Interestingly enough, preaching from the lectionary does not limit one's sermons nor place one in a narrow straitjacket. The lectionary preacher will find tremendous freedom and, above all, variety in his or her sermons. Most of us, if we review our sermons, find that we have pet themes, "hobby horses" we ride, and issues that dominate our preaching. The lectionary forces us to look at a more fully-orbed gospel. Sections of Scripture that have been neglected will need to be considered, unused themes will need to be addressed, overlooked issues will rise to the fore, and the preacher will find that the sermons will have greater variety than previously. The unfortunate dichotomy between personal and social preaching can often be bridged because the lessons in a given year force the preacher to consider the gospel in all of its aspects.

Ecumenically, the lectionary reminds us that we are not alone. It is both comforting and heartening to know that the Scripture we are using on Sunday, in a gathering of either twelve or twelve thousand, is also being used by Christians all over the world at the same time. We sometimes lose sight of the worldwide community of Christians as we work in our own parochial areas, but the universality of the church and the historic unity of the body of Christ can come alive in the worship when we recognize that these same lessons are being read and proclaimed by brothers and sisters in the church universal.

Locally, of course, the use of the Bible makes the pulpit a teaching instrument for the congregation. They are getting exposure to the Scripture and can even be encouraged in adult classes to structure their own studies around the lessons that are also proclaimed from the pulpit. We often assume that our people are schooled in Scripture, but that is not true now, if it ever was. They may wish to be, and they certainly often want their preachers to preach biblically, but as far as knowing the Bible, they do not. What is said of the people can often be said of the preacher. The teaching function of the pulpit for the people can be the same for the preacher. The lectionary gives a planned year-by-year study for the preacher, not only in the preparation of sermons but for systematic study of the Scriptures as well. With such a plan before one, there is benefit both for the study itself and for the sermons that result. Such long-range planning can be of inestimable help to the preacher—and the people.

Above all, the lectionary opens the Scriptures to the preacher at the devotional level, as well as the homiletical or exegetical level. Though it would be difficult for the preacher to separate homiletical study from devotional study, the latter is certainly enhanced by the systematic reading of Scriptures. The sermon often grows out of that personal struggle with Scripture through dialogue, argument, overhearing a word, study, and involvement. The study desk becomes an altar, and the constant preaching from the Scriptures can nourish the interior life of the preacher as well as bring to fruition sermons that arise from the depths of one's being. Above all, and certainly consonant with the worshiping community's intent, the lectionary encourages the preacher to take seriously biblical preaching. Though seemingly obvious from the ordination vows and what has been said about the pragmatic use of the lectionary, there is no assurance that the reading of the Scriptures for the given Sunday will bring forth a sermon evolved from any of the readings. Sometimes a text will be given by the minister but often superimposed upon an already written sermon. As has been pointed out, there may be a schizophrenic relationship—a sermon at war with the text. However, rightly viewed, the lectionary may be the occasion for the preacher to do serious biblical preaching in a systematic manner.

The first thing to be said about biblical preaching—and perhaps the last thing to be said also—is that one's theological stance in regard to the Bible determines how the Bible is used in preaching. That may go without saying, but to state it reminds us that we are in a pluralistic church with a variety of views toward the Bible and its authority. It also suggests that those of us who teach and write in the area of homiletics need to avoid the tendency to be over-prescriptive both in comments on the Bible and particularly in its use in preaching. For example, the preachers who believe that the Bible is *the* Word of God in the literal sense and have a view of its inerrancy have sermons which reflect that posture. Often these sermons are highly rationalistic and structured; e.g., "Five Steps to Salvation," "Building a Meaningful Prayer Life." Sometimes the sermons are constructed apart from the Bible, and the Scripture passages are used as proof texts. The mere citation of the Scripture is its own authority because it is the Bible that is used as proof, support, or illustration.

On the other hand, there are those who, if they refer to the Bible at all, use it as a source book or make a text a motto, or use the Scripture as merely illustrative material. These are the so-called "topical" preachers. Though it would surely be an embarrassment to both, the so-called Bible preacher mentioned and the topical preacher who sees the Bible as *a* Word have more in common than they would wish to admit. The topical preacher, too, is often rationalistic and sometimes has a completed sermon in search of a text. Or, the text may be simply a springboard for a sermon on a theme which the text suggests—a pretext for the sermon idea. Another group of preachers has been affected by the biblical and theological renaissance which occurred roughly after World War II. These preachers tend to see the Bible not as the literal Word of God nor simply as a source book of faith. They do not confuse words with Word. The Bible is truly a holy book, not because it is the literal Word of God but because it *contains* the Word of God. It is salvation or holy history (*Heilsgeschichte*). These preachers often preach biblical ideas or themes (exodus, eschatology, exile, redemption, kerygma) apart from specific lessons, texts, or passages.

The Bible preacher, the topical preacher, and the theme preacher by no means exhaust the list of possibilities for the variety of sermons reflecting specific theological orientation. Theological background does affect both the authority and specific methodology of a sermon. Remembering the admonition about being too dogmatic for all of the Christian strains of the church, there is still a great deal of commonality among Christians in regard to the importance of Scripture. For one thing, the Bible is a book of data which contains our history. It tells us who we are as Christians. To put it another way, it is our story. We cannot tell who we are without it. Also, it is crucial to the worshiping community along with the cross, the baptismal font, the pulpit, and the altar as a means of worship. Further, most denominations in ordination ceremonies ask their ministers to preach the Word, administer the sacraments, and interpret the Scriptures. Devotionally, too, the last is efficacious not only for preachers but also for the people of God.

What then can be said about the Bible for preaching definitions and methodology? Surely, it has an authority for the worshiping Christian, it does tell the story of our heritage, and it does reveal to us God's work in history. Rather than *containing* the Word of God, it might be more accurate to say that the Bible *mirrors* that Word or serves as a translucent means of revealing the Word. One always remembers Luther's dictum that the Bible is the manger where the Christ child is laid. The preacher will find the Scripture viable if it makes a claim on him or her. This is more than an existential relevance which can be quite private and personal. It is more like saying that the Bible becomes Word when it claims us, when it addresses us. That is not passive in the least. It may result in struggle, questions, and even anger, but it is not simply a dispassionate source book. It must be above all meaningful first to the preacher, if it is to be meaningful to someone else. One way to look at biblical preaching is to say that the minister is proclaiming what has become Word to him or her, so that it may become decisive Word for the congregation.

Is there a more specific definition that can be given for biblical preaching? Definitions are dangerous, often personal, and too prescriptive for all. Besides, we do not preach definitions; we preach sermons. Perhaps one can suggest touchstones, signposts, or guides that will give some direction for preaching from the Bible. For one thing, the sermon should preach the good news. What that means will vary, but historically the central gospel message has clustered around the life, teachings, death, and resurrection of Jesus Christ. Those events, often called simply the Christ Event, in one way or another inform or illumine the sermon that purports to be Christian. Whether this kernel of Christian faith be called the good news, the gospel, the salvation occurrence, the Christ Event, or the *kerygma*, that message is the backdrop for the sermon, whether it is explicit or implicit. Two cautions are necessary. (1) To state what has often been called *kerygma* (what God has done and continues to do in Jesus Christ) as either the climax or the conclusion of a sermon does not necessarily make the sermon either biblical or Christian. There may be a tendency to assume that stating the words is the same as the message itself or that oral affirmation baptizes the sermon and makes it the gospel. Such a view leads to a kind of verbal gnosticism whereby one believes that if the right words are uttered the gospel has been proclaimed. (2) The preacher may assume that the *kerygma* is a static body of knowledge which is affirmed and then assented to or denied by the listeners. Contrariwise, the gospel is not a set of beliefs which one assents to or rejects. The preaching of the gospel is tied to the gospel itself. That is, the telling of the story is part of the story. The medium is inextricably tied to the message. The bringer is part of what is brought. The good news is dynamic and alive—not static and dead.

If the first word about biblical preaching is that one way or another it proclaims the gospel, the second word is that it does so through specific Scripture. Work with the lectionary, of course, immerses one in the lessons for the week in a most specific way. There is another more compelling reason, though, for moving from text to sermon. Preaching about the Bible or ideas from the Bible often seems abstract and rationalistic. Personal involvement in the Scripture passages not only enables one to appropriate the message but also to have a discourse in one's own speech with narrative, story, parable, and pictorial language which is reflected in so much of the Bible. A sermon on Psalm 139, for example, will have a dramatic and pictorial style in a way that a doctrinal sermon on the nature of God will not.

We hasten to add, however, that the oft-heard sermon, which has a long beginning with a kind of wooden exegesis and then finally an adaptation of the message to the present day, is not what is meant by biblical preaching. The Scripture passage and message can permeate the sermon without the placement of "Bible material" being a factor. One can preach *from* the text or *to* the text. Indeed, one need not use biblical language to preach a biblical sermon. Charles Rice once stated that we should "think theologically, speak non-theologically."[3] We can study and think biblically but not necessarily use the language. The key is that the sermonic insight has come *from* the passage rather than being read *into* it. It has been said that we make the same point in our day that the Bible writers were making in theirs. The setting, clothes, history are all important in the exegesis, but the sermon need not reflect a biblical lecture in order to be biblical, let alone to be effective. In order to understand the message, however, we involve ourselves with the passage in a specific way, so that we may see if the message that was revealed in that passage is relevant for us today.

If biblical preaching, then, is proclaiming the good news through specific Scripture, it is neither biblical nor relevant unless it is related to contemporary life. That seems so obvious that it is painful to state it, but the fact is that just as the Bible often does not really get preached, so also it often is not related to the life of the people in the twentieth century. This problem is related to the age-old one of the personal versus the social gospel. The Bible is pietistic, otherworldly, and irrelevant, and certainly much preaching reveals that approach. There are some, also, who preach the "now" going from topic to topic and issue to issue apart from biblical categories. The truth is that the sermon's application is part and parcel of the hermeneutical task. The Bible is a historical book, and its revelations came into specific situations, and they still do. Unless the text is applied, it is certainly not biblical.

It is extremely difficult to place specific parameters around biblical preaching which will include all of the aspects of preaching. However, a sermon which proclaims the good news of the Christian message, reflecting the insights arising from the passage read in the service, and applying them in an arresting manner to our personal and corporate lives in the world, could be said to be "not far from the kingdom" (Mark 12:34) when it comes to biblical preaching.

12

The World
and the Word

The historical and traditional picture of the pulpit, vividly portrayed by Herman Melville in *Moby Dick*, remains forever indelible in our minds. Father Mapple's chapel was a lofty pulpit without stairs, but appropriately enough for a ship's chapel, it had a perpendicular ladder at the side. The preacher pulled the ladder in after him when he ascended, "leaving him impregnable in his little Quebec."[1] It became a self-contained stronghold, with its physical isolation signifying the spiritual withdrawal from all worldly ties and connections.

The pulpit was shaped like the front of a ship, and what could be more meaningful: "for the pulpit is ever this earth's foremost part; all the rest comes in its rear; the pulpit leads the world ... Yes, the world's a ship on its passage out, and not a voyage complete; and the pulpit is its prow."[2] This picture of the pulpit—visually and symbolically—seems strangely antiquarian in our day, though there are undoubtedly those who find that image attractive, both theologically and homiletically.

It would be more accurate to search for an image that reflects the tension between the church and the world. Certainly there is a danger of trying to live Christianly in a world without the fellowship of the church. Theodore Wedel once remarked that "even revolutionary armies need a base and a supply of recruits."[3] There is, however, the corresponding danger of cutting ourselves off from responsibility to and for the world. Though a massive subject in itself, the church and the world can be viewed through the prism of preaching and the pulpit. The church cannot cut itself off from the world and its problems and be true to its prophetic tradition, which is part and parcel of its preaching. This is no time for escape and withdrawal, especially in the name of personal piety. Indeed, the piety and the prophetic actually go hand in hand.

As J. C. Hoekendijk reminds us, "Apostolate in our situation presupposes that ecclesiastically one is willing to enter no-man's land."[4] No matter how enticing it might seem to retreat from the preceding turbulent decades—religiously as well as politically—we do so at the peril of losing our mission. The church that fails to reach out passes out. This is not some vague political concern for social action but a theological mandate by the very nature of our call to be Christians.

Karl Barth stresses this point strongly in his discussion of the Christian's call to community and the Christian community giving itself for the world. "The community of Jesus Christ is for the world. . . . The community of Jesus Christ is itself creature and therefore world."[5] And in another place, "Called out of the world, the community is genuinely called into it."[6] In this light, even Father Mapple's ancient pulpit as the foremost part leading the world does not seem so quaint.

Preaching in our world means, among other things, that the process of translation is an imperative—not alone for the world—but even for those in the community whose mental screens are blocked by the biblical and theological language. It may mean, for example, that we continue to preach biblically but without the language—making sure, however, that language reductionism is not theological reductionism. Karl Rahner affirms that we often have to start with the old expression of a theological statement and then return to it, but it has to be "translated" in the body of the sermon, and such a translation can, . . . form the main part or even the whole of a sermon if it is to be intelligible and credible.[7]

The sermon of tomorrow may be one with disguised, if not wholly different, language.

At the same time, the pulpit—if it is to be a viable force now and in the future—must speak forthrightly to the time in which we live and to the issues which we face. The social gospel has a bad connotation in the present day, though the church is not overburdened with activists. Relatively few ministers have had to leave their churches because the gospel they preach is too stringent. We need to be wary of self-styled martyrs who use their pulpits as platforms and embrace controversy either for personal political reasons or for ego trips. But at the same time, the danger is just as real—if not more so—that in our age the broadsides against the activist can be our excuse for the "great cop-out," no matter how pious our rationalizations. For most of us it may be that the lines of the old nursery rhyme will become our battle cry:

"Pussy-cat, pussy-cat,
 Where have you been?"
"I've been to London
 To look at the Queen."

"Pussy-cat, pussy-cat,
 "What did you there?"
"I frightened a little mouse
 "Under the chair."[8]

We desire, at the end of our ministries, to be able to look back at the turbulent times in which we have lived and say more than, "Well, I frightened a couple of mice." We may at least endeavor to clarify issues in the light of the Christian gospel, so that our people can sort out their own Christian witness.

Oliver Tomkins, the Bishop of Bristol, in discussing the so-called generation gap, remarks that

Part of the reproach of the young generation who went to protest marches, as boys and girls emerged from their shared sleeping-bags, was that the older generation, which was very dogmatic about sex, lapsed into confused silence about war.[9]

Whatever our future and whatever the issues, we do a disservice to the gospel to assume that its exegesis does not reach into the lives of people in this world. Ours is an incarnational religion, and biblical faith itself is historical—meaning among other things, our history. We may well consider as a text the words from a young college student who said he was not interested in the church but was impressed with Jesus. When he was asked "Why?" he replied, "He put his body where his words were." That is a text full of judgment for the church and its preachers.

At any rate, we have made too much of a dichotomy between the world and the church. We Protestants have always felt nervous about natural theology. Gerard Manley Hopkins, the poet, has a word which pushes our minds off into the arena of the world. "God's utterance of Himself in Himself is God the Word, outside Himself in this world. This world then is word, expression, news of God. Therefore its end, its purpose, its purport, its meaning, is God, and its life or work to name and praise Him."[10] This idea is expanded by Karl Rahner in a mind-stretching article called, "Secular Life and the Sacraments." The sacraments are seen as the manifestation of the holiness of secular existence, and Rahner affirms that "we ourselves are able to understand properly what we normally call liturgy only from this liturgy of the world."[11] What he says about the mass could easily be thought of in terms of worship and proclamation. The worshiper "hears and speaks in the Mass the Word of the self-revealing God, conscious that this word is the verbal declaration of that other Word which God speaks in uttering the World as his own Word. . . ."[12] He goes on, "It *is* possible, then for someone to see the Christian Mass as the miniature sign of the world's Mass, a world to which Christ himself, obviously belongs."[13]

Rahner's views here are related to his concept of the anonymous Christian, which he spells out in other places. Essentially he means that

the person who grasps God's grace as the radical meaning of his own life has already said yes to the definitive historical appearance of this grace in Jesus Christ, whether or not he knows explicitly that God has in fact given the definitive pledge of Himself in history in this Jesus.[14]

Though the concept of the anonymous Christian raises interesting questions in regard to evangelism and may seem to be imperialistic toward other faiths—even those who consciously desire to be non-Christian— my main concern is to affirm Rahner's view of the community of believers being a part of the world which God has created and filled with grace. Any attempt to isolate church proclamation from speech to the world should be protested. A narrow faith which possesses *kerygma* but lacks *didache* is irrelevant at best and verbal gnosticism at worst. The attempt to separate confession from apologetics must be resisted by the Christian preacher. To proclaim the Word apart from the milieu of the world, which is its setting, is the worst kind of fideism.

On the other hand, precisely because the world and church are intertwined, the world needs to hear the proclamation, and not alone for apologetic reasons. The apologetic task is not so much a rational defense of Christianity or an aggressive determination to enlist all for Christ, as it is a confession, a witness to what God has done, continues to do, and will do to fulfill promises. In short, we are not describing two sermons, two different messages, two specific gospels, two kinds of good news, or even two kinds of audiences. The sermon is confessional to all who hear. For the nonbeliever, it is the constant recall to faith and renewal of commitment. The style of preaching may vary, the occasions may differ, the mode and purpose may change, but the essential kernel of the gospel which defines the preaching of good news is the same old story. We can no longer easily separate the recipients of the message into believers and unbelievers, churched and nonchurched, sacred and secular, "insider" and "outsider."

James Sellers, in his perceptive book *The Outsider and the Word of God*, describes the audiences Christian communicators used to face. On the one hand, there was the audience of the nonadherents, the unbelievers, the pagans. On the other hand, there was the audience of Christians—faithful and believing. With the first, the purpose was to present the gospel as a strange new way of life and urge entrance into the church. With the second audience, the preacher was to "spur and revive lagging faith." Now, says Sellers, there is no two-lobed audience. "The church today actually faces, in nearly every congregation and community, a new audience which is made up almost wholly of *outsiders to faith*."[15] Besides, there are at least two kinds of outsiders: one, the person who claims to be an "outsider" but is a "hidden" Christian and, the other, who claims to be a Christian but is a "hidden" outsider. Sellers refines his definition of the outsider in order to give an understanding to the communicator of his or her role in determining the purpose and response sought in preaching. "I have used the term 'outsider' to cover all who turn deaf ears to the message of the church—both the church attenders and the nonattenders."[16] In short, we have one gospel, one message, one arena. We may talk of church and world as separate entities metaphorically but certainly not literally.

However, the church continues the struggle with the world and has always had ambivalent relationships with its culture. Richard Niebuhr, in his classic study of the relation of the church to culture, suggests four stances which the church has maintained throughout its history.[17] First, Christ against culture, which has been the church's attempt to see itself, if not against culture, at least apart from it. The other extreme has been the Christ of culture, in which we tend to identify "our way of life" with Christian values. Other positions in between are more moderate: Christ above culture, in which Christ enters culture to transform it; Christ and culture in paradox, in which the Christian is in a continuous dilemma and duality between the world of Christ and the world of culture; Christ transforming culture, in which the Christian lives in the world and attempts to convert both humans and society. Though these paradigms may not be all-inclusive, they certainly do suggest that the church has a relationship to culture and that this relationship is often decisive for the hearing and receptivity of the gospel. To keep Melville's figure in mind, whether the pulpit is the prow or the bow, the preacher is vitally affected by the culture in which the word is preached.

Specifically, this has two extremely significant aspects which affect preachers particularly. One is their own relationship to culture, both as a broadening aspect of their lives and as a way of meeting their apologetic task by being exposed to cultural forms. The second is more specifically the role of the preacher in his or her prophetic role as a spokesperson both within and to the culture. Whereas Niebuhr's categories may pertain to church and state, culture can also be considered in other forms, e.g., art, literature, music. In the second, it is surely concerned with the Christian in the state. In either case, the preacher lives in that culture, and to ignore it is to invite irrelevancy.

Paul Tillich, perhaps more than any other theologian, was the one who brought religionists into a viable relationship with the culture. His definition of religion as that about which we have ultimate concern broadened our understanding of the religious task in relationship to the world in which we live (religion is the substance of culture, culture is the form of religion). He tended to diminish the gap that has existed between the sacred and the secular. In his own words he writes that the

> character of this concern implies that it refers to every moment of our life, to every space and every realm. The universe is God's sanctuary. Every work day is a day of the Lord, every supper a Lord's supper, every work the fulfillment of a divine task, every joy a joy in God. . . . Essentially the religious and the secular are not separated realms. Rather they are within each other.[18]

The world of the arts serves as one example which commands the attention of the preacher who wishes to be sensitized to helpful expressions of culture. Tillich alludes to these art forms as keys which reveal our predicament in the present world and in the world universally.

In particular, and to limit the scope, literature provides a prism through which the arts and culture can be refracted for the preacher. There are several reasons why an art form such as literature can be helpful to the minister. For one thing, we have seen that our ethos includes competence, integrity, good will. Apart from the fact that breadth of reading adds to competence, such exposure also sensitizes our nature, thereby deepening our authenticity and integrity. It also makes us more universally aware of people's needs, which is necessary in creating good will toward those entrusted to our care. In short, the broader the person, the better the specific preacher. Broader should not suggest shallow, but preachers are persons before they are ministers, and literature is one way to widen interests and knowledge—hence, heighten character. In America we are spiritual descendants of Benjamin Franklin in many ways. We are instrumentalists and pragmatists. We are looking for solutions, helps for Sunday, and aids for work in the church. It is difficult to see that reading *The New Yorker* may be as important as reading a Bible atlas. In some ways the preacher should resist the temptation to choose the useful over against the beautiful. Americans as pragmatists have always been nervous about "art for art's sake," but with the idea of the preacher's exposure to culture and the world, it is precisely that neglect of the arts that has fostered our in-house siege mentality.

As we have already seen, in Tillich and others, there are theological reasons for being concerned with cultural expressions. As to literature, it is clear that many authors speak more realistically about our situations than do our preachers. They often reveal persons as they are, not as preachers want them to be. Even if the writers' visions of the contemporary human drama are faulty, it is important for us to know what they think the human condition is. Often, they have a more realistic view of the actual situation than do we as ministers. The pulpit is always tempted to answer questions no one is asking. If, however, as Tillich says, the culture and gospel interpenetrate through the method of correlation and if that which is ultimate reality is religious, then culture may provide answers as well as questions.

Protestants, particularly, have been criticized for not having a doctrine of natural theology, and that is one of the primary reasons for not having an interest in the arts. The indictment may be too strong, for there is a strain of theological concern for God's presence in the process of creation and in the natural order. Many of the present-day movements in theology give credence to the so-called "worldly" expressions which were the scourge of Puritanism. The world is our arena, as well as the church, and theologians as diverse as Rahner and Tillich are at one with that view. Karl Rahner's view of the "anonymous" Christian certainly sets the mandate for the church in the world. In our day, the blurring of sacred and secular seems as natural and providential as the separation once did to theologians. Bonhoeffer's "religionless Christianity" has spoken to a multitude of Christians who face the culture with Christian faith. Though there is no universal agreement, it does seem significant that in the present the questions that arise in religious faith are often more anthropological than theological. Essentially, then, culture and church, whatever label is used, are related theologically, and that relationship may bring from the side of culture answers as well as questions. If revelation is still a meaningful term, then that seems entirely appropriate in an incarnational religion. Literature as one of those cultural expressions furnishes us not only an aesthetic experience but also an insightful one religiously as well.

Though authors might rebel at the thought, they are often writing "theological categories," whether consciously or not. Whether it is intended or not, literature is replete with the concepts of "sin" and "grace," and not always because religionists are prone to "read into" literature these categories. Sometimes an author may be demonstrating non-faith, but *Deus absconditus* can be considered a theological category. As preachers we may decide there is more analysis than soteriology, but Christians should not ask an author to do our work. It would be interesting to speculate what would happen if T. S. Eliot had written a third act to *The Death of a Salesman*, but we should be grateful for Arthur Miller's insight into the human condition with that classic play. Theology is our job, not the author's or playwright's.

Yet, many writers do reflect the gospel "anonymously." One play of Miller's, *All My Sons*, raises explicitly the theme of guilt. A novel such as Robert Penn Warren's, *All The King's Men*, can be seen through the old biblical text, the wages of sin is death. Golding, in *Lord of the Flies*, and perhaps in all of his work, can be seen as wrestling with the doctrine of original sin. John Gardner, in a book on writing itself, *On Moral Fiction*, is most explicit in affirming that *love* should be both the basic theme and method for writers. None of these examples even includes the number of writers both in and out of the Christian faith who are intrigued with the figure of Jesus Christ as a subject for novels, poetry, art, and music.

There are literary reasons for being attuned to culture through literature. As we have seen in regard to language and style, writers are plumbing other modes of literary expression than what is usually heard from our pulpits. Narrative and description, for example, get a larger play in writing than the argumentative and didactic styles of preachers. In writers, the idea is often dramatized, as effective speaking wonts to do. Their style can be multileveled and existential. Indirect discourse can be replete in the effective writing style found in our best novelists and playwrights. Though the writers may not be convinced religionists, and their plot and language may seem too "earthy" for some, it is clear that they are attempting to portray life as it is. The preachers should not ask authors to "play in our ball diamond." Enough to ask is a realistic portrayal of life, and we can bring the gospel to bear as appropriate. The Bible itself is most realistic about humans' proclivity for sin, thus we need not ask authors to be hermetically sealed from their world of reality. So-called "religious" literature is not much help to the minister. So much that is labeled such is neither good literature nor good religion. Actually, many of the so-called secular writers are "moralists" in their own right. A Samuel Beckett, for example, in his seemingly near hopeless plays, always maintains a love for the creatures he creates. A love for, and sympathy with, our human scene is often the mark of contemporary writers whom we too easily regard as merely secular.

Besides the aesthetic, theological, and literary reasons which literature provides as a mirror of culture, there is no denying the resource values for the preacher. Though we have warned against the pragmatic as the sole reason for reading, it is clear that a by-product of absorbing oneself in the arts is the mammoth reservoir of materials which will be at the minister's disposal. We should not be afraid of the Christian prism we see through when we read literature or are exposed to the arts. Artists, as we know, deal with religious ideas and people as their subjects. The preacher can see moral and religious values, even when the artist may not. The minister, then, will not feel guilty if illustrations, ideas, and sermon themes come bounding out of the pages of a book as the fallout from reading and study. It is not a question of going to literature as avaricious and hungry preachers seeking "morsels" for Sunday morning. Rather, it is as post-resurrection Christians who are sensitive to our cultural milieu.

If one way the minister takes the culture seriously is typified in literature as a paradigm of the arts, a more prevalent way is through the way he or she deals with controversial issues from the pulpit.[19] It is at this point that the church and the culture intersect most vividly. Unfortunately, for some this is no problem. They attempt to separate the personal gospel from the social gospel, forgetting that ours is a historical religion, and apart from history it is meaningless. Yet, there are those who attempt to compartmentalize faith and "stick to the gospel and stay out of politics." Many of these, however, do end up "politicizing" the gospel, but under some other heading, such as "moral values" as interpreted by the particular preacher. All preachers have the temptation to become "Rev. Chameleons," blending in with the culture and lifestyles of their congregations. We all want to be liked, if not loved, by our people. It is difficult to be prophetic with our friends. For some, as has been said, their motto is "Come weal or come woe, our status is quo," or to paraphrase Teddy Roosevelt, "Speak softly and carry a big feather." For these preachers, the cross on the church steeple has been replaced by the weather vane, and the gospel that is preached is determined by whichever ways the political winds are blowing in that particular parish.

Still others wish the social aspects of life did not impinge on the gospel. They are often the ones who compartmentalize their faith. They like to look at life through a rearview mirror, looking backward to a Bonanza-land when everything was peaceful. My father once said that Adam and Eve were the only persons he knew of who did not sit around and talk about the "good old days." It was Halford Luccock who observed that when Rip Van Winkle went to sleep the sign over the tavern door had a picture of George III, King of England. When he awoke, there was a picture of George Washington. He had slept through a revolution, and many of us wish we could do that. Knowing we really cannot, preachers often get depressed, seek other employment, or grit their teeth and stay in, helped along with Seconal, Gelusil, Maalox, and perhaps prayers.

Others seek martyrdom. They consider the prophetic the only note that can be sounded, and become like drunken Don Quixotes, tilting at every windmill that comes along, usually turning any issue into their "pet cause." These preachers move from church to church, unfortunately considering themselves martyrs for the cause. Fosdick, probably the greatest social preacher in the twentieth century, warned against preachers who turn their pulpits into platforms and their sermons into lectures, thereby ignoring their people. Camus, that wistful religionist, once commented that "too many people now climb onto the cross merely to be seen from a greater distance, even if they have to trample somewhat on the one who has been there so long."[20]

Although preachers respond in a variety of ways to controversial issues, which may be biblical or theological as well as social, the question most of us face is how do we preach on vital issues effectively? Those who have written on the subject tend to simplify the ways into *direct* and *indirect*.[21] For those church bodies who do not follow a lectionary—and even some who do—there is a thematic or program year as well as a Christian year. Often, alcohol and drugs, community, peace, and other social expressions get an emphasis one way or another. Though there is a great deal of merit in holding up live issues for treatment in the pulpit, from the standpoint of both strategy and substance, there are problems. For one thing, laypersons can have negative reactions just from the announcement itself and stay home or come out of loyalty to the pastor and be inured against the subject in advance, knowing full well they will not have to hear about it again for another year. Such a stance also lets the minister off the hook. Even in the days of segregation, ministers could preach on race relations once a year, and congregations often indulged the minister in that privilege, knowing that the preacher was following the wishes of some general church entity. Strategically, then, such a direct approach may set up defenses in the congregation before the sermon begins, defenses which are difficult to overcome. As to substance, the program year is often at variance with the Christian year, so that the preacher has the difficulty of opting for one or the other. In many instances, even the conscientious social preacher will stay with the Christian year.

Yet, the special days are one significant way to deal directly with controversy. Another is the absolute candor method. This seems on the surface to be the only honorable way to deal with a difficult issue—to address it directly and depend on the fair-mindedness of the congregation to hear and possibly to be convinced. Some very effective social preachers take this approach, and its effectiveness depends in the final analysis upon the ethos of the preacher. Persons are usually more hostile to the ideas than to the preacher, and if they accept him or her, then they will listen. A preacher who is an effective pastor can preach directly and effectively with this open and candid approach. We have seen, though, that there are unskilled martyrs who may put the cause before the people and fail miserably. Also, in the absolute candor approach, we may assume the congregation is where we wish they were rather than where they really are. Understanding of one's congregation is especially decisive in controversial preaching. Another danger with the direct and absolute candor method is that the gospel may be obscured by the issue. The preacher may be preaching on a subject and treating it psychologically or sociologically rather than theologically. Those sermons often create negative reactions from congregations, not alone because of the issue, but because the preacher may be in fields in which members of the congregation are more conversant than the preacher. Yet, if the minister is a good pastor and has an outstanding ethos, then he or she may be persuaded that a direct approach to controversy through announced themes and with absolute candor is the only effective and honorable way to preach.

The indirect method, on the surface, seems less honorable. We have already mentioned preachers who ignore controversy. Some in the name of preaching the Bible may hide behind that and say they are either giving implications or permitting the parishioners to draw their own conclusions. Granted the danger of being too oblique in addressing social issues, there are some merits in approaching the issues indirectly. For instance, one could be preaching on gospel themes week by week and through illustrations in those sermons give examples that impinge directly on the controversial subjects. Actually, the person who is preaching from the lectionary, let us say, emphasizing biblical and theological themes, is in a better stance strategically. The preacher is in his or her area of expertise, and having that platform, it is then easier to draw the implications on a given issue from the perspective in which one is well versed. Thus, from the standpoint of strategy, the preacher may think that the more controversial the subject, the more expository the sermon. In addition, for the lectionary preacher especially, if the biblical framework is the normal stance, then introducing a social or theological controversy will not seem an intrusion but the natural extension of the gospel when applied in our daily lives.

Whatever direction the preacher takes toward controversial preaching, there are some principles that would be well to keep in mind. Great social preachers have usually followed many, if not all, of these guidelines. First, keep the controversy in the context of the gospel. If it cannot be addressed in light of the gospel, then there may be a question as to its fitness for the pulpit. Second, and alluded to earlier, the more controversial the subject matter, the more expository one can provide. Third, get as many facts as possible before dealing with a controversy, particularly if it impinges on areas where the preacher feels shaky. Generalizations and verbal broadsides without support can be counterproductive to thoughtful listeners.

Use the pronouncements of one's church. Most of the church bodies have issued statements on principles or have adopted stances in regard to major issues. This kind of authority adds to the credibility of a preacher's position and gives credence to pulpit pronouncements. Such statements, particularly in connectional churches, have an authority which goes over and beyond the preacher's. As in the case with normal pulpit speech, the indicative is better than the imperative. Unless handled well, the imperative can become angry and argumentative. In controversy, especially, the more positive one can be in the pulpit, in language as well as demeanor, the more effective will be the sermon and its reception. The preacher must recognize honest differences. There are sincere Christians who may look at issues differently and who will stand in opposition to the preacher's understanding of both the gospel and the controversial issue. To recognize these differences not only shows understanding of the congregation in front but also will reflect a fair-minded Christian in the pulpit dialoguing with them. And, above all, speak truth in love. Scolding, or angry words and attitudes will do little to change minds, and even less to induce response to the message of the gospel.

The preacher stands in the midst of a culture that cannot be ignored. Though there may be some who believe they can live in a Gothic ghetto with a private vocabulary talking to others of like mind and call that the Christian church, it is clear that the church at its best has never been a refuge from the culture in which it finds itself. Though it is true that Christian preaching is in a liturgical setting to a congregation of adherents, these Christians are in the world and so is the preacher. Since the culture impinges on the people of God and since those people impinge upon their culture, the Christian pulpit may be our central way of influencing and changing the culture.

Notes

1. Theology of the Word

1. T. H. L. Parker, *The Oracles of God* (London: Lutterworth, 1947), p. 20.
2. Martin Luther, *Commentary on Genesis*, vol. 1 of LUTHER'S WORKS, ed. Jaroslav Pelikan (St. Louis: Concordia, 1958), p. 157.
3. Theodore O. Wedel, "Is Preaching Outmoded?" *Religion in Life* (Autumn 1965): 545.
4. Walter M. Abbott, ed., *The Documents of Vatican II* (New York: America, Association, Herder and Herder, 1966), p. 155.
5. Ibid., p. 180.
6. "The Articles of Religion of the Methodist Church," *The Book of Discipline of The United Methodist Church* (Nashville: United Methodist, 1980), par. 68, art. 13, p. 58. Cf., "For wherever we find the word of God purely preached and heard, and the sacraments administered according to the institution of Christ, there, it is not to be doubted, is a Church of God" (John Calvin, *Institutes of the Christian Religion,* trans. John Allen [Philadelphia: Presbyterian Board of Christian Education, n.d.] vol. 2, bk. 4, ch. 1, sect. 9 [281]).
7. *An Ordinal: The United Methodist Church.* Adapted for official Alternative Use by the 1980 General Conference. Prepared and edited by the Section on Worship, General Board of Discipleship. Published by The United Methodist Publishing House. Copyright © 1979 by Board of Discipleship, The United Methodist Church, p. 37.
8. Ibid., p. 49.
9. William H. Willimon, *Integrative Preaching*, ed. William D. Thompson (Nashville: Abingdon, 1981), p. 13.
10. H. Richard Niebuhr, *The Meaning of Revelation* (New York: Macmillan, 1941), pp. 21–22.
11. Ibid., p. 177.

12. Fred Craddock, *As One Without Authority* (Enid, OK: Phillips University, 1974), p. 108.
13. Dominico Grasso, *Proclaiming God's Message* (Notre Dame, IN: University of Notre Dame, 1965), p. xxxi.
14. Gerhard Ebeling, *The Nature of Faith* (Philadelphia: Fortress, 1961), p. 191.
15. Thomas Oden, *Pastoral Theology* (San Francisco: Harper, 1983), p. 137.

2. Preaching's Debt to the Old Testament

1. A. E. Garvie, *The Christian Preacher* (New York: Scribner's, 1921), p. 24. To be fair to Garvie, a later book, *The Preachers of the Church* (New York: Doran, 1926), shows more of a relationship between Old and New Testaments in regard to preaching, even though that connection is shown only in relationship to the prophetic strain, which raises problems considered in this chapter.
2. Edwin C. Dargan, *A History of Preaching* (Grand Rapids: Baker, 1970), 1:21. Cf., "But while preaching belongs specifically to Christianity, it has an ancestry which can be traced, and that ancestry is in the Old Testament" (John Ker, *Lectures on the History of Preaching* [London: Hodder & Stoughton, 1889], p. 15).
3. T. Harwood Pattison, *The History of Christian Preaching* (Philadelphia: American Baptist Publication Society, 1912). Pattison especially scorns Gibbon who speaks of the uniqueness of the Christian orator: ". . . this is rather the sneer of the partisan than the statement of the historian" (p. 1).
4. Yngve T. Brilioth, *A Brief History of Preaching*, THE PREACHER'S PAPERBACK LIBRARY (Philadelphia: Fortress, 1965), p. 4.
5. A. Cohen, *Jewish Homiletics* (London: Cailingold, 1937), p. 3.
6. Dargan, *History of Preaching*, pp. 15–16, 19–20. See also John Albert Broadus, *On the Preparation and Delivery of Sermons* (New York: Harper, 1944), pp. 6–10.
7. Broadus, *Preparation and Delivery*, p. 12. Cf. Dargan, *History of Preaching*, pp. 18–21.

8. Ker, *Lectures*, p. 20. C. S. Horne, *The Romance of Preaching* (New York/Chicago: Revell, 1914), pp. 51ff., begins the prophetic (preaching?) tradition with Moses. A modern scholar, H. H. Rowley, *Worship in Ancient Israel* (Philadelphia: Fortress, 1967), p. 70, while not writing specifically about preaching, places Moses in the prophetic tradition.

9. Cf. Andrew Bruce Davidson, *A Dictionary of the Bible*, ed. James Hastings (New York: Scribner's, 1898–1904), p. 757 for a discussion of the prophetic tradition.

10. Broadus, *Preparation and Delivery*, pp. 10–11. A. S. Herbert, *Worship in Ancient Israel*, ECUMENICAL STUDIES IN WORSHIP, no. 5 (Richmond: John Knox, 1959), p. 41, presents the dichotomy this way: "Provided we do not press the antithesis too far, we may see the priest as presenting Israel to God and the prophet as presenting God to His people." The problem is that we usually do press the antithesis this far.

11. Davidson, *Dictionary of the Bible*, p. 757.

12. Rowley, *Worship in Ancient Israel*, p. 103; cf. pp. 150ff.

13. Pattison, *Christian Preaching*, p. 11. Herbert's statement in note 10 above is also applicable here.

14. Rowley, *Worship in Ancient Israel*, p. 152.

15. Ibid., p. 163.

16. Ibid., p. 224.

17. Herbert, *Worship in Ancient Israel*, p. 31. Brilioth seems to take a different approach: "The synagogue, having arisen as a substitute for the temple, originated cultic forms of a wholly different character" (*Brief History*, p. 2).

18. Brilioth, *Brief History*, p. 2.

19. Ibid., p. 3. Brilioth contends that preaching's relation to the synagogue is more obvious but less profound than its relation to Old Testament prophecy.

20. W. O. E. Oesterly, *The Jewish Background of the Christian Liturgy* (Gloucester, MA: Peter Smith, 1965), p. 37.

21. Ibid., p. 99.

22. Pattison, *Christian Preaching*, pp. 9ff.

23. Rowley, *Worship in Ancient Israel*, p. 242.

24. Hans Lietzmann, *The Beginnings of the Christian Church*, trans. Bertram Lee Woolf (New York: Scribner's, 1937), p. 197.

3. Preaching's Debt to the Greeks and Romans

1. Dietrich Ritschl, *A Theology of Proclamation* (Richmond: John Knox, 1960), for example, denigrates rhetoric and considers its influence harmful. Other more recent writers disparage rhetoric by assuming it as the cause of rigid forms and structures and rationalistic discourse. Such a simplistic analysis overlooks the influence of scholasticism at a later period and the varieties of classical rhetoric at an earlier one.

2. Dargan, *History of Preaching*, pp. 14–19.

3. Although the names and specific teaching are of little importance for our purposes, there are many others who made significant contributions to the field of rhetoric. For example, Corax, who defined rhetoric as the art of persuasion and who named the five parts of a discourse; Protagoras, the father of debate, who was a grammarian and who recognized the two sides of every question; Gorgias, a skeptic who was adept at sweetness in words and created a new style in prose writing.

4. Alfred Croiset and Maurice Croiset, *An Abridged History of Greek Literature*, trans. George F. Neffelbower (New York: AMS, 1970), p. 283.

5. Cf. B. Jowett, trans., *The Works of Plato* (New York: Dial, 1936).

6. It is interesting to note that Aristotle, who is considered so often to be related to the Christian tradition through St. Thomas Aquinas, is connected with the tradition of rhetoric which became allied with the development of preaching. We see this more clearly in the fourth century when rhetoricians became Christian leaders, e.g., St. Augustine.

7. C. S. Baldwin, *Ancient Rhetoric and Poetic* (Gloucester, MA: Peter Smith, 1959).

8. Hartwig Thyen, *Der Stil der Jüdisch—Hellenistischen Homilie* (Göttingen: Vandenhoeck & Ruprecht, 1955).

9. Saint Augustine, *On Christian Doctrine*, trans. D. W. Robertson, Jr. (New York: Liberal Arts, 1958).

10. Brilioth, *Brief History*, pp. 8–10.

11. R. W. Dale, *The Atonement* (London: Congregational Union of England and Wales, 1905), p. 107.

12. Rudolf Bultmann, *Theology of the New Testament* (New York: Scribner's, 1951), 1:3.

13. Ibid., p. 33.

14. C. H. Dodd, *The Apostolic Preaching and Its Developments* (London: Hodder and Stoughton, 1951), pp. 3ff.

15. Ibid., pp. 25–28.

16. Victor Paul Furnish, "*Kerygma* and *Didache* Reconsidered," *The Perkins School of Theology Journal* (Winter 1961):31ff.

17. J. B. Weatherspoon, *Sent Forth to Preach* (New York: Harper, 1954), especially ch. 3.

4. Words as a Medium of God's Presence

1. Roy V. Wood, "Centennial Address," *Second Century Celebration, May 11–12, 1979* (Evanston, IL: Northwestern University, 1979), pp. 1–4.

2. See Marshall McLuhan, *Understanding Media* (New York: McGraw-Hill, 1964).

3. Frank Dance, "Communication Theory and Contemporary Preaching," *Preaching* 3, no. 4 (1968):29.

4. Frank E. X. Dance, "Toward a Theory of Human Communication," *Human Communication Theory*, ed. Frank E. X. Dance (New York: Holt, Rinehart, and Winston, 1967), p. 290.

5. Quoted in Susanne K. Langer, *Philosophy in a New Key* (Cambridge, MA: Harvard University, 1951), p. 63.

6. Brendan Gill, "The Theater," *The New Yorker*, 7 March 1983, p. 110.

7. Dance, "Toward a Theory," p. 300.

8. Ibid., p. 301.

9. Ibid.

10. Walter J. Ong, *The Presence of the Word* (New Haven: Yale Uni-

versity, 1967). This important book comprised the Terry Lectures of 1964. Father Ong provides at a deeper level the concerns which Marshall McLuhan simply probes.

11. Langer, *Philosophy*, p. 126.
12. Dance, "Toward a Theory," p. 289.
13. Karl Menninger, *The Vital Balance* (New York: Viking, 1963), p. 139.
14. Paulo Freire, *Pedagogy of the Oppressed* (New York: Herder and Herder, 1970).
15. Gerardus van der Leeuw, *Religion in Essence and Manifestation*, trans. J. E. Turner (New York: Macmillan, 1938), p. 403.
16. Frederick J. Streng, "The Function of 'Sacred Word' in World Religions: A Phenomenological Approach" (an unpublished paper), pp. 2–3, 8.
17. Charles E. Winquist, "The Sacrament of the Word of God," *Encounter* 33, no. 3 (Summer 1972):229.
18. Ibid., p. 222.
19. Quoted in Winquist, "Sacrament," p. 224.
20. Ibid., p. 229.
21. William L. Malcomson, *The Preaching Event* (Philadelphia: Westminster, 1968).
22. Ebeling, *Nature of Faith*, p. 188.
23. Ibid., p. 26.
24. John McKenzie, "The Authority of the Word," *Preaching* 4, no. 4 (October–November 1960):20–29.
25. Amos Wilder, "The Word as Address and the Word as Meaning," *The New Hermeneutic*, NEW FRONTIERS IN THEOLOGY, ed. James M. Robinson and John B. Cobb, Jr. (New York: Harper, 1964), p. 212.
26. H. H. Farmer, *Servant of the Word* (New York: Scribner's, 1942), p. 27.
27. Ibid., p. 51.
28. Kyle Haselden, *The Urgency of Preaching* (New York: Harper, 1963).
29. Archibald MacLeish, *J.B.: A Play in Verse* (Boston: Houghton Mifflin, 1956), pp. 130–131.

5. Using the Bible Biblically

1. Among others the following are very helpful: Ernest Best, *From Text to Sermon* (Atlanta: John Knox, 1978); James W. Cox, ed., *Biblical Preaching* (Philadelphia: Westminster, 1983); James W. Cox, *A Guide to Biblical Preaching* (Nashville: Abingdon, 1976); Leander E. Keck, *The Bible in the Pulpit* (Nashville: Abingdon, 1978); William D. Thompson, *Preaching Biblically* (Nashville: Abingdon, 1981).
2. Lloyd R. Bailey, "From Text to Sermon: Reflections on Recent Discussion," *Quarterly Review* 1, no. 2 (Spring 1981):8.
3. Ibid., p. 5.
4. For the term *interpretive paraphrase*, I am indebted to my colleague, Kent Harold Richards, and students in a seminar at Iliff, which was taught jointly under the title, "From Text to Ministry."
5. Craddock, *As One*, pp. 45, 105.

6. From Study to Sermon

1. Martin Esslin, "The Theatre of the Absurd," *On Contemporary Literature*, ed. Richard Kostelanetz (New York: Avon, 1964), pp. 204–221.
2. Roger Copeland, "The 'Linear' Play Still Retains a Powerful Potential," *The New York Times*, 21 August 1983, p. 68.
3. Ibid., p. 69.
4. Ibid., p. 180.
5. Willard L. Sperry, *Reality in Worship* (New York: Macmillan, 1925), p. 282.
6. Dr. Grobel was a colleague at the Vanderbilt University Divinity School. A sample of his method appears in my *Proclaiming the Word* (Nashville: Abingdon, 1964), pp. 57–58.
7. The sermon was preached at the First Baptist Church, Evanston, IL.
8. Martin Luther, *Lectures on Deuteronomy*, vol. 9 of *Luther's Works*, pp. 7–8.

7. Forms That Allow Movement

1. Phillips Brooks, *Lectures on Preaching* (New York: Dutton, 1902), p. 5.
2. McLuhan, *Understanding Media*, ch. 3.
3. Brooks, *Lectures on Preaching*, p. 44.
4. Haselden, *Urgency*, p. 42.
5. Quoted in Dargan, *History of Preaching*, 2:115.
6. Kendrick Grobel, "The Practice of Demythologizing," *Journal of Bible and Religion* 27, no. 1 (January 1959):28–29.
7. Nathaniel Hawthorne, *The Scarlet Letter* (New York: Pocket, 1974), p. 236.
8. Craddock, *As One*, p. 108.
9. Dodd, *Apostolic Preaching*, p. 7.
10. Ebeling, *Nature of Faith*, p. 6.
11. Oden, *Pastoral Theology*, p. 131.
12. Ernest T. Campbell, "They Also Serve Who Lead," *The Princeton Seminary Bulletin* 2, no. 1 (New Series 1978):5.
13. Quoted in Leslie J. Tizard, *Preaching* (New York: Oxford University, 1959), p. 41.
14. Eduard Schweizer, *The Good News According to Matthew* (Atlanta: John Knox, 1975), p. 239.
15. Martin Buber, *Tales of the Hasidim: The Early Masters* (New York: Schocken, 1947–48), p. 17.
16. Klaus von Bismarck, "The Christian Vocabulary: An Obstacle to Communication?" *The Ecumenical Review* 10, no. 1 (October 1957):13.
17. Willimon, *Integrative Preaching*, p. 37.

8. How Shall They Hear Without a Preacher?

1. See Charles L. Bartow, *The Preaching Moment* (Nashville: Abingdon, 1980); Clyde E. Fant, *Preaching for Today* (New York: Harper, 1977); Ronald E. Sleeth, *Look Who's Talking* (Nashville: Abingdon, 1977) and *Persuasive Preaching* (Berrien Springs, MI: Andrews University, 1981).

2. I am indebted for this insight to Natalie Sleeth, my wife, who is a well-known composer of choral music.

3. Quoted in James Atlas' review of Mark Harris' biography of Saul Bellow, *Saul Bellow: Drumlin Woodchuck* (Athens, GA: University of Georgia, 1980). Taken from *The New York Times*, 16 November 1980, C17.

4. Fant, *Preaching for Today*, ch. 8.

5. See note 1 above for examples.

6. Harry Emerson Fosdick, "What Is the Matter with Preaching?" quoted in *Pulpit Digest* (September–October 1983):298.

7. There are textbooks in both homiletics and speech which give specific attention to introductions and conclusions.

8. Quoted in C. S. Lewis, *Beyond Personality* (New York: Macmillan, 1945), p. 49; Lewis borrows this parable from George MacDonald.

9. The Sermon Event: Preaching

1. Craddock, *As One*, uses objective/subjective in a somewhat different way.

2. Cf. Sleeth, *Persuasive Preaching, Look Who's Talking*; Craddock, *As One*.

3. Craddock, *As One*, pp. 70–71.

4. Grasso, *Proclaiming God's Message*, pp. 222–232.

5. Edmund Hill, ed., *Nine Sermons of Saint Augustine on the Psalms* (New York: P. J. Kenedy and Sons, 1959), p. 23ff.

6. James E. Sellers, *The Outsider and the Word of God* (Nashville: Abingdon, 1961).

7. For a more detailed study of the congregation, see Sleeth, *Look Who's Talking* and *Persuasive Preaching*.

8. Further discussion of these concerns is found in Sleeth, *Persuasive Preaching*, pp. 9–21.

9. Contemporary books on pastoral care and psychology as well as some which deal with the relationship of the pulpit and counseling are invaluable at this point.

10. The Sermon Event: Hearing

1. Craddock, *As One*, p. 112.
2. Augustine, *Christian Doctrine*, bk. 4.
3. Ibid., sect. 9.
4. Pablo Casals and Albert E. Kahn, *Joys and Sorrows* (New York: Simon and Schuster, 1970), p. 60.
5. Edwin Newman, "Language on the Skids," *Reader's Digest* 115, no. 691 (November 1979):41–45.
6. Jack L. Stotts, installation charge to Professor Donald M. Wardlaw upon his installation as James G. K. McClure Professor of Preaching and Worship at McCormick Theological Seminary, May 17, 1979.
7. Roger Fallot, "Down the Up Staircase," 3 February 1982 (unpublished sermon).
8. Oden, *Pastoral Theology*, pp. 130, 131.
9. See Sallie McFague TeSelle, *Speaking in Parables: A Study in Metaphor and Theology* (Philadelphia: Fortress, 1975), pp. 20–22 for a more detailed analysis of Keen's "The Peach-Seed Monkey."
10. Janice Riggle Huie, "Preaching Through Metaphor," *Women Ministers*, ed. Judith L. Weidman (San Francisco: Harper, 1981), p. 52.
11. C. S. Lewis, *Miracles* (New York: Macmillan, 1947), p. 88.
12. Ibid., p. 90.
13. Lewis, *Beyond Personality*, p. 40.
14. Ibid., p. 41.

11. Language That Serves God

1. Ronald E. Sleeth, "Wrestling with God's Angel," *Circuit Rider* 5, no. 1 (January 1981):14–15.
2. A more exact rendering of Bultmann's thought would be the interpretation that Grobel attributes to him: "To a true Lutheran there are no 'great preachers' but only responsible and less responsible ones" ("Practice of Demythologizing," pp. 28–29).

3. Charles L. Rice, *Interpretation and Imagination* (Philadelphia: Fortress, 1970), p. 90.

12. The World and the Word

1. Herman Melville, *Moby Dick* (New York: Signet, 1956), pp. 55–56.
2. Ibid.
3. Wedel, "Is Preaching Outmoded?" p. 535.
4. J. C. Hoekendijk, *The Church Inside Out* (London: SCM, 1968), p. 64.
5. Karl Barth, *Church Dogmatics* (Edinburgh: T & T. Clark, 1962), IV, 3, 762.
6. Ibid., p. 764.
7. Karl Rahner, "Demythologization and the Sermon," *The Renewal of Preaching: Theory and Practice*, CONCILIUM 33 (New York: Paulist, 1968), p. 21.
8. *The Real Mother Goose*, illustrated by Blanche Fisher Wright (Chicago: Rand McNally, 1916, 1944), p. 26.
9. Oliver Tomkins, *Guarded by Faith* (London: Hodder and Stoughton, 1971), p. 111.
10. Gerard Manley Hopkins, quoted in *A Hopkins Reader*, ed. John Pick (New York: Oxford University, 1953), pp. xiii–xiv.
11. Karl Rahner, "Secular Life and the Sacraments," *The Tablets* 225, nos. 6822 and 6823 (March 6 & 13, 1971):236ff., 267f.
12. Ibid.
13. Ibid.
14. Ibid.
15. Sellers, *The Outsider*, p. 13.
16. Ibid.
17. H. Richard Niebuhr, *Christ and Culture* (New York: Harper, 1951).
18. Paul Tillich, *Theology of Culture* (New York: Oxford University, 1959), pp. 40–41.
19. Cf. Sleeth, *Proclaiming the Word*, ch. 6.
20. Albert Camus, *The Fall* (New York: Knopf, 1959), p. 114.
21. See Harold A. Bosley, *Preaching on Controversial Issues* (New York: Harper, 1953).

Index